"Marva Bailer is an inspiration to everyone she meets. She is constantly working to uplift others and has a positive outlook on life and the people she meets. In this book, she shares her secrets to this optimistic internal engine. In these trying times, this is just the insight we all need."

—**Becky Blalock**
Speaker and Best-Selling Author of Dare
Award-Winning C-Level Executive and Board Member
("We Are the Champions" by Queen)

"Marva is a true servant leader. She always looks for the positive in every situation and the good qualities in each person. We are partners and soul sisters who work together to support and uplift women in the technology community we serve. She is a great friend, mentor, and leader."

—**Patti Dismukes**
Vice President of Professional Services, HUNTER Technical
Chairman of the Board, Women in Technology
("I Am Woman" by Helen Reddy)

"When you FAIL, it really is your 'first attempt in learning.' I am inspired by Marva's drive to succeed and do well, regardless of the obstacles in front of her. She used her personal experiences to excel and really focus her passions."

—**Vicki Wright-Hamilton**
Author of Game Face
Award-Winning Technology Executive and Advisor
("Try Again" by Aaliyah)

"[Marva is] always so incredibly professional and perceptive in how [she] thinks about leadership, motivating teams and collaborating for success. This book highlights that thinking and couldn't be more timely given the current environment. There is something in it for everyone—a seasoned leader or a new manager. The practical advice and tactical suggestions are relevant in every business context. I can't wait to use our walk-up songs more regularly. What a fun and engaging way to connect with each other!"

—Allen Mueller
CEO, Emissary.io
("Let's Get It Started" by the Black Eyed Peas)

"Marva Bailer makes the art of storytelling as approachable and engaging as she is, delivering in *Be Unexpected* a creative collection of real world–tested, specific strategies for communicating with each other in today's post-pandemic, virtual-meeting world. She will inspire you to turn those boring online meetings into genuine opportunities to connect with your clients, colleagues, and friends."

—Maryfran Johnson
CEO, Maryfran Johnson Media, Host of "CIO Leadership Live" Video Series and Podcast. "Boardroom Bound" Columnist, CIO.com
("Beautiful Day" by U2)

"Marva is strength, freedom, and authenticity. Her love and passion for pushing for positive impact, connection, and real communications is empowering. She makes decisions and connects from a place of love, awareness, and integrity. Powerhouse!"

—Penny Collins
President and CEO, Women in Technology
("I Am The Fire" by Halestorm)

"Origin stories matter, and they are the foundation for who we are, what we do, and how we become. It is energy that will sustain relationships during hard times. It is important for me to feel the energy of others before I can trust them. As a former professional baseball player, I have had the benefit of having a walk-up song that gave me the energy that I needed before a competitive at-bat against opposing pitchers. My walk-up song is "Welcome to Atlanta" by Jermaine Dupri. It has a fast beat, strong bass, and descriptive lyrics about "My Atlanta" that I was born and raised in as an African American male. The song reminds me to be authentic and fully present in all spaces that I am in. If I am in the space, I belong in the space and everyone present should feel my presence. It reminds me to be unapologetic and self-confident, recognizing that when I have self-confidence based on prior successes, simple things that I can do that appear complex can actually get done with excellence and speed."

—*C. J. Stewart*
Former Chicago Cubs Baseball Player, Cofounder and CEO, L. E. A. D.
("Welcome to Atlanta" by Jermaine Dupri)

"Unfortunately, conformity is pervasive in the business world, limiting the potential of professional interactions, events, meetings, and careers. Marva's energy and personality are infectious, and those traits shine through in this book as a way to inspire all of us to step out of our comfort zones and exceed expectations. *Be Unexpected* is a must-read for anyone seeking to motivate their teams, advance their career, and stand out in a world of look- and sound-alikes."

—*Curtis Brooks*
Principal, Magis Group
("September" by Earth, Wind & Fire)

"*Be Unexpected* is a fun read that is full of creative ways to improve personal influence and enjoyment. Marva is a master at connecting with others, and her book shows us why."

—*Russ Rausch*
CEO and Cofounder, Vision Pursue, LLC, Performance Mindset
("Twice as Hard" by The Black Crowes)

"Marva is about as genuine of a human being as you can get. She is a true professional with a passion for helping others. Go figure. Do people actually help other people these days without wanting anything back in return? Yes, they sure do, and Marva is a testament to that. She is also a transparent leader that is not afraid to leverage her story and her own personal experiences to inspire and educate others. This is what makes her special, and combined with her career experiences, it's what makes her a BRAND."

—*Nick F. Nelson*
CEO and Founder, Brandpreneur
("The Big Payback" by James Brown)

"I've always taken a nontraditional path in everything that I do in life. My intention is to help and serve others, keeping in mind that anything is possible. When I met Marva, she was an inspiration and 'breath of fresh air' as someone who has created their own path despite the odds and inspires everyone she interacts with. She has an energy and compassion to her that never seems to have a day off. I couldn't be more proud and excited for her lessons and inspiration to touch others that haven't had the privilege to engage with her. Marva is the definition of a positive 'change-maker,' and I can't wait for the world to see through this book!"

—*Shaina Shiwarski*
Founder and Technology Executive
("I Want to Break Free" by Queen)

"I originally met Marva as a customer, which quickly turned into a great friendship. In my entire sales career, she's still the only person who walked me out of a sales meeting with her company and offered to give me coaching feedback on the spot. Not only was it invaluable, it shows her character and how she has a never-ending need to help lift up those around her. Her energy is infectious and acts as a homing beacon of inspiration for those within her circle."

—Kevin Gillies
Global Sales Leader, Key Accounts, LinkedIn
("Kickstart My Heart" by Mötley Crüe)

"On a professional level, Marva's 'Finding Your Voice' message to our IT team was inspirational and thought-provoking. I have never had so many positive comments from our team about a guest speaker as we did after Marva's presentation. As a father of three teenage daughters, Marva's message struck a personal cord with me, as well. I showed my daughters the video from our IT all-hands meeting, which led to some great father/daughter discussions on how they can find their voice!"

—David Cutter
Technology Executive, Oldcastle/CRH Americas Materials
("Kashmir" by Led Zeppelin)

"Some people are just natural connectors, but she might as well be Master Connector of the Universe. Listen to her philosophy of connecting people and giving back. It's astonishing."

—Stu Heinecke
Author, How to Get a Meeting with Anyone
("Smoochin'" by Mark Knopfler)

"Marva's style, personality, and flair make her immediately likeable and someone you want to know. I had the privilege of reading *Be Unexpected* early and did so in a single sitting. Although my intent was to read a few pages and finish over the next week, once I began, I could not quit. As a sales and marketing executive for almost fifty years, this book is gold. I highly recommend *Be Unexpected* to anyone wanting an advantage in business from one of the hardest working, truly sincere executives in our country and across the planet."

—*Ricky Steele*
Author of The Heart of Networking
("Man in the Mirror" by Michael Jackson)

"Anyone who has met Marva knows that her energy lights up the room. She's an innovator, a connector, a coach, a partner, and a fearless female leader who is never afraid to disrupt the status quo. When I first met Marva in New York City in 2018, I was instantly inspired by her positive energy. She had this pointed ability to get even the most hesitant person in the room to think differently in a way that left them feeling empowered. It's easy for any of us to fall into a dated routine, present lackluster content, and avoid change. It's much more of a challenge to break away from what's comfortable and test out new and creative approaches. Marva does an impeccable job of inspiring people to show up, try something new, and have fun doing it. As an aspiring female leader, I'm so lucky to have gotten to partner with and learn from Marva for two-plus years and will look to her for inspiration far into my future."

—*Taryn Pahl*
Account Relationship Manager, Key Accounts, LinkedIn
("Don't Stop Me Now" by Queen)

"Marva infuses creativity and fun doing things differently with outcomes that will wow people!"

—*Jean K. Holley*
Corporate Board Director, OneSpan, Herc Holdings, and Accord Financials
("I'm Still Standing" by Elton John)

BE
UNEXPECTED

BE
UNEXPECTED

Resetting Routines to
Revolutionize the
FUTURE OF WORK

MARVA BAILER

BOOKLOGIX
Alpharetta, GA

ISBN: 978-1-6653-0149-7 - Paperback
ISBN: 978-1-6653-0150-3 - Hardcover
eISBN: 978-1-6653-0151-0 - eBook

Library of Congress Control Number: 2021923036

The opinions of this book are the author's and do not represent the position or opinions of Splunk Inc. or any present or former employer.

Printed in the United States of America   0 2 1 1 2 2

♾This paper meets the requirements of ANSI/NISO Z39.48-1992 (Permanence of Paper)

Author photos taken by Nick F. Nelson

In honor of my parents, who gave me the love of reading;
my grandmother for the art of conversation;
and my family—my husband, Don, and our kids,
Heather and Patrick—for their support and love.
You are my biggest cheerleaders.

//////////////////// **CONTENTS**

///////////////////// *FOREWORD*

What makes a person or event unforgettable? Why are some experiences so compelling, while others are just ho-hum? It's a crucial question in business. It's also relevant to our personal lives.

We've all experienced people whose words sear into our brains forever. We've also experienced individuals who prattle on and no one remembers a word they said. The people and events that prompt us to fully engage, the moments that cause us to sit up and take notice, are the moments when we experience something unexpected.

Being unexpected is the key to standing out in a cluttered world.

Experiences become more memorable when they break an established pattern. When something (or someone) changes the frame, it disrupts our expectations. It is this very disruption that causes us to pay attention. Interestingly enough, you don't need to be extravagant, or even charismatic, to be unexpected. You simply need to break a pattern and step out of the usual ho-hum. Sometimes even the smallest tweaks can have a dramatic impact.

I've known Marva Bailer for several years; she is memorable, she is engaging, and her discussions leave people wanting more. She has mastered the ability to "be unexpected."

What's most fascinating to me is how Marva creates unexpected magic in a traditional business setting. In this book, she shares simple actions and ideas that you can use to make your own interactions and events more engaging, more exciting, and more memorable.

From innovative ways to use music to questioning techniques that light up the attendees' frontal lobes, Marva's insights will help you become more personally compelling. They will also help you better engage with others.

I've watched Marva light up a room, transform webinars from background noise into emotionally engaging experiences, and take video-conference screens full of customers from apathetic to inspired. What many of us long referred to as "the magic Marva elixir" has now been translated into practical techniques every leader can use to up the engagement with your team and customers.

As you read this book, think about all the forgettable meetings, uninspired events, and the endless conference calls that you've been forced to endure. These events are more than just boring; they sap our energy and they waste our time. This book will help you break out of that malaise and become that unexpected breath of fresh air that people need.

The time you and your colleagues spend together should be invigorating and inspiring. It should be an opportunity for rich connection, creative idea generation, valuable insights, and strategic action. Whether you meet in-person or via video call, your time—and your colleagues' time—is a valuable and nonrenewable resource.

In Be Unexpected, Marva Bailer shows you how to make the most of this precious time.

—**Lisa Earle McLeod**
Author of *Selling with Noble Purpose*
2021 Top Global Guru for Sales
("Dancing Queen" by ABBA)

This book will give you **COURAGE**, **CONFIDENCE**, and a **SPIRIT** to engage with others in a positive environment that creates mutual trust and shared experience.

///////////////// *INTRODUCTION*

I f we spend approximately one-third of our lifetime at work, how can we make the experience not only mutually beneficial, but productive, positive, and interesting? Time is precious and an area where we lose attention, move fast for growth, or miss being in the present moment.

In the sea of personality, psychometric, and leadership assessments, the Hermann Brain Dominance Instrument (HBDI) assesses our thinking preferences. Most of the people I collaborate with on a daily basis are "high blue," which is a strength of logical decision-making using data, which can include statistical data or past experiences to make decisions. Unique to my current field of work, I am an idea person, a "high yellow" on the HBDI scale. I mention this assessment as well as other data, such as this input, as recognition that we are not all wired the same in how we present, communicate, and retain information. I share this continued awareness as it continues to strive to improve the workplace for diversity, inclusion, access, and equity. These assessments provide transparent indications that highlight the differences in decision making, energy, how you work under stress/pressure, leadership styles, emotional intelligence in addition to other indicators. I share my personal experience as a statement that through comparison, I have succeeded and thrived in my profession, but through these indicators, I am typically the outlier of the rest of the group. The headline here is diversity of thought and approach is a highly discussed topic in boardrooms and companies and is valued for growth and innovation as well as deeper and broader connections with customers and communities they serve.

And since we are sharing personality assessments, the first assessment I took in school was the Myers-Briggs Type Indicator, created by the work of Isabel Briggs Myers. These personality, design quality, stressor, and motivator tests are generally available at no fee. As a result, they are utilized widely starting in high school to nonprofit and volunteer organizations as well as corporate settings. The comfort level of sharing data and being vulnerable so others can interact with us in a more positive and productive manner is a great advancement in this field.

My first high-tech role out of college required sales people to take this test in addition to a background check, and they used it as a condition of employment. Human Resources policies will not support that practice in these times, but it shows the connection to business. Just this last month as I was in final editing of the book, our son asked us, as a family, to do this test to better understand each other. I was asked by a Millennial CEO during a board of directors interview, where I landed in both cases to appreciate and understand the other person's perspective and energy. I remember it being a very long test issued by a formal assessment center, and was apprehensive. I was pleasantly surprised to take it for free online with great info on the sixteen different personality types. I am an "ENFP-A." This test, Enneagram's, StrengthFinders 2.0, and associated leadership- and personality-based assessments are popular and discussed broadly in social situations and business. It is great to see this use of data created a century ago relevant in twenty-first-century society.

Some of these ideas I outline will be obvious and simple, and that is the point. As we go through our daily life, we often are moving so fast, we recognize key areas of our process that are distractors, multipliers, and productivity diminishers. In this book, I share insights and stories bridging generational and diverse teams. This content has been tested on groups from underrepresented communities, interns, engineers, multimillion-dollar sales professionals, academia, and even military personnel.

Going through life as a redhead, you are always noticed for the right reasons and the wrong reasons. With no place to hide, you adapt. Most people wait a lifetime to retire and then get to do what they love. I was fortunate to have sponsors that recognized I could make my passion my actual job and could qualify and repeat my actions into something that could be articulated, shared, and taught to others to adopt. That was a challenge and then a blessing. I had the opportunity to analyze the process, the environment, the emotion, then share and observe, and ask for feedback.

Each chapter outlines one or two key areas for you to test

in your company, your team, your classroom. I encourage experimentation and observation of the energy, sentiment, and outcome.

This book will give you courage, confidence, and a spirit to engage with others in a positive environment that creates mutual trust and shared experience. I will share quotes, songs, and stories that are motivating and memorable, and look forward to hearing your stories.

To frame and set the stage for our time together, the Roman philosopher Seneca said,

"The whole future lies in uncertainty:
live immediately."

I am going to live immediately. Being vulnerable and authentic, the time is now.

B - BRING

E - ENERGY

To the Expected

B - BRING

E - ENTHUSIASM

To the Expected

B - BRING

E - EMPATHY

To the Expected

Burst out of the comfort zone with *"Intentional spontaneity"* to bring change and joy.

1

START WITH A SONG

Music gives a soul to the universe,
wings to the mind,
flight to the imagination,
and life to everything.

Plato

What if every meeting, every conversation, every video call started with the same energy as a sporting event? Think about it for a minute: How do you feel when they start playing music in a stadium or coliseum? The crowd is alive with energy, interest, and desire to find out what is next. That simple act of starting with music brings positive energy. What if that same principle could be applied to our daily lives?

In this chapter, I will outline simple, tangible ideas for you to leverage to create positive, fun, and memorable ways to lead off a meeting. Whether a formal business review or a session with interns, or even a kickoff to a virtual classroom session, you want to ignite the energy. We will discuss simple and engaging ideas for you to try. That is the key operational word, "try," a.k.a. "experiment." The core theme with the ideas outlined in this chapter is personal engagement, trying to get to know the person on the other side of the camera or table as a person up-front before you get into the conversation. This approach has a bidirectional effect with the sender and receiver. The sender needs energy and confidence to make that connection with the receiver.

I encourage you to think of past meetings, interactions, and conversations, and replay in your head how the outcome may have changed if the suggested below was applied. I refer to this concept as "intentional spontaneity," or the anticipation of bursting out of the comfort zone, creating change and joy.

What Is Your Walk-Up Song?

Let's start with the "walk-up song." You know, the music played before a presenter at an awards ceremony or baseball game walks out? Just asking yourself or the presenter, "What's your walk-up song?" at the start of a meeting will result in a positive physical reaction. Even if you don't play it, you will notice yourself truly thinking about the answer. It could be a gut feeling or a song that has kept you going for the week. It could be something very strategic to shock your audience or bring dialogue. Or, it could be one that has truly worked as a motivator and confidence-builder for you over a long period of time.

I observed this playing out in a positive manner in a virtual setting by participating in a customer advisory board. The CEO started with this exercise of sharing walk-up songs. This approach did not disappoint. One hundred percent of the participants shared their songs (we did not play them). The meeting owner and I prompted them to share why they selected their particular song, and the thinking-out-loud process was fascinating. We were quickly brought into stories of their teenage years, times of challenge, passions for causes, where they grew up, and more. This connection got the participants to engage right out of the gate. This data point was referred to throughout the meeting, tying into topic areas. In addition, it helped match a face to a name, and at the end of the meeting the host even had a contest for the most memorable song.

Fast-forward a week. Will the participants remember what they said at this exercise? Yes! And will there be a positive thought process? Yes! That is the outcome we really all desire in most work circumstances: high performance and connection of the people involved with continuous learning and curiosity.

In researching the origin of this practice, we find it rooted in the American pastime, baseball. During the early 1970s, Nancy Foust, MLB organist, switched from playing the traditional "Take Me Out to the Ball Game" crowd-pleaser when players came up to bat. Instead, Foust started playing customized songs for each of the players to get them energized. The idea of the "walk-up song" stuck. It continued to change throughout time and evolved, giving us concrete results that show there is a positive effect on those who utilize it.

Consider these three data points: a professional musician, an actual field study of a professional baseball team, and one of my own personal experiences in a business setting. These three examples illustrate how walk-up music enhances the motivation of the "performer" and the energy felt from the "audience." These examples further illustrate the positive memories associated with performance when music is played. These strong positive memories can propel power and action, in addition to boosting confidence. If you think about it, you are enhancing and optimizing your surroundings to support your performance.

Tiffany Jenkins, BBC contributor and host of the highly successful internet show *Juggling Jenkins*, shared her personal experiences of the connection of music to a point and time in your life: "This is an experience shared by everyone: Hear a piece of music from decades later, and you are transported back to that particular moment, like stepping into a time machine." She shares primary research on memory and music that is applied to dementia patients. She summarizes the topic by sharing her song "Rhythm is a Dancer." Jenkins shares the feeling created by her song as framing a mantra for her life. She goes on to call this song the "soundtrack of her life."

The discussion and sharing of a walk-up song is fun and

engaging, but it is a window and glimpse into someone's life, opening the door for more authentic and connected relationships. Supporting the sentiment, David Gockley, general director of the San Francisco Opera, explains how the music can bring us back to memories that propel power or action: "Well-composed music can conjure feeling, location, and circumstances in the flash of several seconds by virtue of what we remember from the past. Music can also express hope and unleash a kind of power."

The second example is a simple yet powerful article on a field study that highlighted a quick change to a walk-up song and the performance improvement of a pro baseball player. A journalist for the Bay Area News Group reported on a field study on a Giants shortstop who "was in a slump last June. The shortstop, Crawford, made some adjustments to his approach at the plate. Namely, he switched his walk-up music to Kelly Clarkson's 'Stronger.' His batting average jumped twenty points in the second half." After reading this story, I have added this song to my start-of-the-day playlist, and it works!

Researching this topic has been fun and has deepened the relationship with friends and colleagues with whom I have trust and rapport. This question of "what's your walk-up song?" brought deep thought, internality, and an engaging conversation. Similar to the references found during the research, the motivation and the inner voice that gets us motivated may not be as others assume. For example, many of the male athletes that unexpectedly have chosen pop female artists—Taylor Swift, Kelly Clarkson, and Katy Perry—as their motivational voices of choice. The topic of music and motivation is part of the team banter and formation. I am collecting a group of stories and insights from this book and speaking engagements. I share the sentiment from CJ Stewart, a former professional baseball player, and he was involved with a leadership session where I encouraged the formal group to start each interview segment with a walk-up song to get personal faster and increase the energy of the session:

"As a former professional baseball player, I have had the benefit of having a walk-up song that gave me the energy that I needed before a competitive at-bat against opposing pitchers. As a public speaker, I have also experienced the advantage of having a walk-up song before I presented to a large crowd in person or [digitally]. My walk-up song is 'Welcome to Atlanta' by Jermaine Dupri. It has a fast beat, strong bass, and descriptive lyrics about 'my Atlanta' that I was born and raised in as an African American male. The song reminds me to be authentic and fully present in all spaces that I am in. If I am in the space, I belong in the space, and everyone present should feel my presence. It reminds me to be unapologetic and self-confident, recognizing that when I have self-confidence based on prior successes, simple things that I can do that appear complex can actually get done with excellence and speed." I encourage you to ask the intentional question of what your walk-up song is and why it generates a vision and connection with the listener.

The third example is from my field observations. I thought, *If this works for pro athletes as they go to work each day, why not apply this principal to a corporate work environment?* So, I did some experiments. I am sharing so you can try it in your companies, schools, or learning centers.

The first was an experiment for a business meeting involving twelve to twenty-five participants. The setting was a quarterly business review. These are formal sessions where reviews, goals, and commitments are set for the future. With distributed work environments, this is often one of the only times the team gets together, and typically the only time during the quarter where they are presenting to their peers. Peer-to-peer presentations can be supportive, but they do have an underlying element of friendly competition.

To execute this idea of the walk-up song, I did the following set up:

- I had selected a DJ from the group ahead of time — a coveted role.
- Speakers attending the meeting provided the allocated DJ with their song preferences. We established a deadline for song choices. Those that missed the deadline were at the mercy of the DJ.
- I provided an audio speaker. Make sure you have a microphone to amplify the sound.
- If doing so virtually, have the music files cued up to play.
- To foster the stage for inclusive energy, everyone arrived in the room with music playing. This simple act increased the energy level and set the tone for the day. As people got their food and settled,

routine set in . . . laptops on, checking email messages, eating food, acting super busy. As a facilitator, you have a few options on how to get the team to be present and pay attention to the speaker, and these are some simple ones to keep people on their toes.

- **Mix up the line-up:** If there are multiple presenters from the same group or topic area, instead of saying, "10:00: Mary, 10:30: Joe, 11:00: Renee," say, "10 a.m.–11:30 a.m.: Group 1" or "10–11:30 a.m. Mary, Renee, Joe (thirty-minute segments)."

For less formal meetings or conversations, you can try these ideas:

- **Who's next on deck? Or, the Batting Line Up?** Call upon people ahead of time. Instead of asking, "Does anyone want to start?" say, "Let's start with Renee, then Mary and Joe are next." This alerts the next speakers to gather their thoughts. I discuss this attention-keeper later in the book. The idea is, who is on deck? Think about a baseball team, swim, gymnastics, or track meet. This approach moves the time along and allows the facilitator to make sure they include everyone they want to hear from during the session.
- **Who's next?** If you want to really keep people awake, another great way to break the routine is to switch up the routine. When the eager, confident

person raises their hand, you call on them and then pause. Make it a *real* pause (count to five in your head), and then at the last minute, instead of them answering the question or taking their turn presenting, you instead have them pick someone else.

That looks like this: You call on Renee, who has eagerly raised her hand, and then you pause. Watch the body language of the group; they will relax. Then ask Renee, "Who would you like to call on?" She then calls on Joe, who was halfway checked out. Now observe the body language. The anticipation and attention builds when a peer is calling on them and it is unexpected who will speak next.

- **Set the energy.** To take this theme a step further, set the stage and engage the dubbed DJ. Be unexpected . . . When each presenter moves to the front of the room to do their part of the meeting, the DJ plays their walk-up song. This simple thirty-second moment breaks the routine of a typical meeting.

As discussed previously, the energy level in the room increased for the audience and the speaker. The speaker gained confidence and the attention was turned to them. The audience felt they were a part of the experience. Learning about others at a deeper level is the goal of high-performing teams and part of supporting an inclusive culture. Sharing the variety of artists prompted conversation.

This theme can be applied to calls and situations where the song cannot be played. The idea is to visualize the memory of the song and make that connection with your audience. In my travels, I have seen this play out with simple creativity. With the switch to a more casual work environment, the chosen wardrobe of many is T-shirts. A good concert tee generates discussion, or when you are using a slide to introduce a speaker, having them in their favorite concert tee generates interest. I, personally, consistently do two things to create immediate interest and informality. One is to have a slide that mentions my song and has a picture of me and the Heart sisters. The other is a picture I have in my office of a signed poster of my go-to artist. It is a great conversation starter, as this conversation or meeting opener is intentional and better than the routine small talk—another topic we will review in more detail later in the book.

I encourage you to ask the intentional question of what your walk-up song is and why it generates a vision and connection with the listener. Many people ask one question and then move on to the next topic. I encourage you to ask a second and third question, diving deeper into the response to gain connection and insight. This will continue the energy and attention you have created by introducing music and a personal aspect to your meeting or conversation. I have seen great success and affinity by using the "walk-up" as a theme and setting for the rest of your session.

One of the biggest challenges of meetings after a break is gaining the attention of the audience. People are engaged in conversation, getting food, making phone calls, and the last-minute bio breaks. In many cases, the break is the only time people get to converse, so they are highly engaged in this activity. Instead of an abrupt admonishment approach, consider leveraging the energy and connection of the participants and getting their attention as a group, indicating something new is about to happen. Music can be leveraged as an indicator that something has concluded and it's time to get to the purpose of the meeting. During breaks, consider playing music. The break in the conversation alerts the participants that something new is occurring. Simple . . . but effective.

This intentional control or set up of the environment you are in is your responsibility wherever possible. Details matter, and they effect the energy and productivity of the interaction. Upfront discussion of these details with the team, and being empowered to make on the fly changes in real time, is critical. Culture is a top priority for most companies; these small changes will set the tone and connection for the team. Most do not think of this simple idea. For large, highly produced presentations, they do, but not for routine meetings, panel discussions, and team-led sessions.

These ideas are simple but may be a disruption or off-script for those organizing the meeting. Depending on the complexity, this can range from a full production crew, marketing or public relations team, executive assistant, or audio-visual leader. I can share from years of experience most people will respond to your requests with "Great idea we will do that next time." Well, what if you do not get to a next time? I encourage you to professionally challenge and offer mutually beneficial solutions that are low risk for both parties. Every session where I have had influence, whether prearranged or not, I go to the back of house (the back room where you are meeting and usually has the audio visual/sound team) and ask them to put on music as the audience enters the meeting. You, as the leader, need to set the tone for a positive experience and assume the risk to make an on-the-fly change. You will be remembered for being creative yet respectful.

"Influence" is the key word. Infusing this personalization/door-opener is simple and can be used even at the last minute. Not everyone likes last-minute, but as disruptive leaders, it is our responsibility to break routines for positive impact. This may be one of those opportunities for you, as long as the ask is simple and respectful, and you are open to just using a phone at the back of house. No need to overthink the music choice, the genre really does not matter; just pick something that is not offensive and has energy. In some cases, I even asked the audio-visual person to play what they liked from their personal collection, which if interesting, I tied to the opening of the presentation.

One of the last two panels I was involved with as a guest and facilitator had a panel of disruptive leaders speak about their life journeys. I introduced this concept of walk-up music to connect with the speakers. It took some convincing, mostly around logistics, but they were agreeable. The first question to the speaker was about why they chose that walk-up song, and the same dynamic occurred: The "politeness" of the listeners became an environment of inclusion and connection.

In both cases, the moderator could see the positive reaction from the audience, and their first question was about why that song resonated with them. You could see the body language relax and the human connection created.

////////////////////

So, what is my walk-up song? Anything by the band Heart; "Barracuda" is the go-to if walking on stage because it is a power-woman song with a great guitar riff.

One of my most memorable moments was meeting Ann and Nancy Wilson, the lead singer and guitarist of Heart, on my fiftieth birthday. My childhood friend and I attended a summer concert. We met the sisters in a VIP experience. It was interesting as we were prepped to meet the celebrities, but the promoter shared that both were shy during one-on-one conversations; we were warned to not talk too much or be over the top. Referencing back to what we learned during the history of the walk-up song, music brings you back to a place, a feeling, a moment. All I could think of while meeting Heart was my fourteen-to-sixteen-year-old self and all the memories from that time of my life: the repetitive nature of playing songs over and over, and then playing on the guitar, using them as inspiration and motivation.

Something came over me when I approached the

women. It was then that I shared with Ann how she was my motivator and the words of her music helped me through my cancer journey. This familiar "stranger," who I will most likely never meet again, was the first person—outside of a small group of family—I shared with out loud that I was fighting breast cancer. I chose not to share on social media or with coworkers and others because of the stigma and bias people hold for those fighting cancer. She had a tear in her eye, and we connected. She showed no judgement, only support to keep at the fight.

During the concert, I felt like they were talking to me, which is consistent with why we are so drawn to artists and their words. We feel that connection to human spirit. As shared in the beginning of this chapter, music can re-create a feeling or motivation.

We want to experience the effectiveness of music for motivation, and the memory of a time, place, situation that generates feelings, in a positive manner. This memory of a time, place, or situation can generate feelings we want to experience again in a new context. I reflect back to the songs of my teenage years that helped me to overcome challenges and the unknown. They have served to inspire and bring confidence for new challenges that life can bring.

I share this with you so you really think about how music does inspire and focus your actions and sets the stage for transparent communication.

Additionally, by intentionally incorporating music as an "instrument" that infuses productivity and brings you to a focused and centered position, you can leverage it when you need that support or inspiration. The keyword here is "intentionality," or self-awareness of the different emotions, focus, and memories the music engenders. Think of this as your theme song. This theme song can be the same as your walk-up song, or one you hold dear to your heart that acts more as a mantra.

My theme song, from another rocker during my teenage years, is "Right Now" by Van Halen. The piano crescendo leading up to the song gets me ready to conquer anything, and the lyrics are like an anthem: "Catch your magic moment. Do it right here and now." Another song, "Drive" by Incubus, stirs emotion that can bring a tear to my eye on the power of overcoming any challenge, being your best, and feeling okay with whatever comes your way. The lyrics are a mantra I live by every day.

As shared in the beginning of this chapter, the intent is to create energy, awareness, and connection. Consider how you have used music in the past or will utilize it in the future to be memorable and positive.

Turn off autopilot, grab the yoke, and make an *acceleration of spin.*

2

EVERY SECOND COUNTS

Don't count every second,
make every second count.

━━━━━━━━━━━━━━━ **Unknown** ━━━

The goal of this book is to provide guidance and inspiration for you to reset the routines of yourself and the teams you lead. In twenty-five years of business and professional meetings, countless conference calls, and over a thousand social and business events, one theme remains constant: We revert to autopilot or a routine.

In the next three chapters, I will illustrate simple actionable examples you can apply to your workplace to enhance communication and connection while having some fun along the way. I encourage you to picture yourself or your team in the scenario and reflect on the positive change in the interaction.

There are countless books and programs on meeting planning, discovery, meeting and agenda control, presentation and engagement enhancement, questioning and overcoming objections, negotiation, time-management, and more. I want to spend most of our time together focusing on one specific area: analyzing how the way you introduce yourself and your team sets the stage for engagement and the energy of the meeting.

I have witnessed time and time again well-executed programs where the first ten minutes were flat. This wastes time, which may not seem like an issue now, but if you follow the trends of communication and business, the two-hour, two-martini lunches are a thing of the past. In the fast-moving global world, every minute counts. In addition, studies are showing that with each evolution of generations, the attention span times are reducing due to opposing factors, increased knowledge, and increased distractions. Studies show that a goldfish has a longer attention span than a human—with the goldfish at nine seconds and humans seven to eight seconds—and are still diminishing.

In 2020, we had a new dynamic in the workplace. Due to the COVID-19 pandemic, people are working remotely. Since mid-March 2020, my days are filled with six to nine hours of video conference calls with cameras on. The days of in-person meetings are put on pause. It is interesting because with most professionals in this mode, it is easy for autopilot to kick in, as well as for distractions to increase. Without that in-person opportunity, the attention-span factor is even more important to consider. Every second matters.

In October of 2020, all of the professional conferences, analyst events, and meetings were moved to virtual. This ranged from large technology conferences with over 200,000 attendees to national industry board and academic sessions. In just one day, I had accepted invitations to my own company's customer conference, an industry analyst firm's conference, two other technology partners' conferences, and that evening was invited to three virtual galas. In watching one company's customer interviews where the interview started off slow, I realized I had the opportunity to fast-forward or choose to exit and watch something else. This is a big difference than an in-person experience, where my normal spot in the room is in the line of sight of the speaker. I would never get up and leave; I would stick it out. In the new virtual world, gaining the attention or support of the audience is more important than ever. Not saying that if the speaker is not a great orator they will always be dismissed; everyone has a talent for connection if they are honest and authentic.

For most of my career, I have been in high-technology sales in leadership. Eighty percent of the time, I notice introductions like, "Hi, I am Devon Smith, your account manager." What does that tell you about Devon? Not much. I believe this polite routine is a social norm that begins in grade school. Students are asked to say their name, age, and grade. I got to see this play out firsthand during a volunteer experience with eight-to-fifteen-year-old students in a virtual entrepreneurial summer camp. Here are a few elements of the camp so you can better understand my point:

- This is their first time meeting each other.
- They are from different schools.
- They are from different parts of the country.
- They are randomly placed in teams with people they may not know.
- They have limited time to come together to create and sell a product.
- It is a competition.
- Everyone must participate and be part of one aspect of the process (i.e. design, strategy, marketing, market research).

With these elements in play and the dynamic of nerves—note, the others on the call are all adults from top technology companies who are serving as judges—what would be a good way to start off the introductions? Some people call this an "icebreaker." I observe, most often, that icebreakers are typically well done and a part of team meetings or conferences. I share these thoughts with you as the prequel, with the design point that all interactions matter, and time and attention are limited.

The students were asked to introduce themselves with the following prompts:

- Name
- Age
- Grade

If you map that back to the aforementioned elements, none of this information clarifies the values or experience of the new team member. Additionally, with the only new data point being age, that aspect could create affinity—an eight-year-old aligning with another eight-year-old. It could also create an unconscious bias, where a fifteen-year-old may feel they have more experience than the eight-year-old on the team.

I noticed as the first students went through the roll call that most mumbled their name or said it quickly, and then put enhancements on their age and grade. Jumping in to quickly disrupt the pattern, eager to experiment my field research on this age group, I made a quick suggestion to say what their favorite product was of the fashion company we would be designing for, or their favorite color, and why. You could tell this element caught them off guard and required more thought than saying their name, age, and grade. There were more laughs and demonstrations of thinking about their answer.

My recommendation is to keep the intro simple, but add one or two elements that provide information to experience (creditability), insight (knowledge), or shared values (affinity). We will dive deep into each of these areas, providing different examples for you to visualize and put into action in your workplace or community.

My suggested rework for this example is for each student to say:

- Their city
- Their name
- Their favorite product from this fashion company

Politeness does not equal *listening* or *connecting.*

Their grade, school, and other details can be shared later.

After each person, the facilitator should repeat their name—"Thank you, Trevor"—and then move on to the next person. We will review the cue-up approach, which is similar to a swim or gymnastic meet, where you indicate the next people "on deck," or, to use a non-sports visual, the next actors for the scene in the play, the next act in a concert, or even the next two people at the department of motor vehicles. The goal here should be to attach a name with a face, to get the person comfortable with the group, and to build trust and affinity.

I see this time after time in the workplace and have developed a process to improve the energy and engagement. Here are my observations from my executive coaching practice's breakout workshop session proceeding a keynote for International Women's Day in London: To get the attention of the audience and set the stage for the workshop, I had them introduce themselves with no prompt. I did not introduce myself further than being teed up by my host. Like the group of teenagers, the audience was polite, but you could tell they were on autopilot with the social norm of introductions.

All the people introduced themselves with:

- Their name
- Their company title, which included acronyms
- How long they had been at the company

I smiled intently, leaned in, and walked toward them as they did their intros, very engaged and positive. After about five people had gone, I stopped the sequence of intros. Then I asked four people on the other side of the room what the last five names were, and not one person could remember them.

What happened? They went on autopilot or routine. People were polite, but not really listening or connecting. And the acronyms may be relevant to a parochial group, but may not translate to everyone. Thus, they can be distracting.

As aforementioned with the teenage example, stating their title can create an unconscious bias, as they may be from a department that may be known for specific expertise. If they say, "I am Susan from Professional Services, director," and the meeting is to develop a new product, some may think Susan does not have experience in that area, when she may have actually had a longstanding career in product development. One hundred percent grounding on role/job title and tenure is great if you are wanting to highlight new people or give credence to longer tenure for experience, but on its own this element does not tell you much and could create unconscious bias. Here is an example of reasons to consider: In some scenarios, a long tenure may indicate tribal knowledge and experience the flip side, which imply part of the old way of doing things and not open to change. Stating a title helps identify the group, authority level, and context, but on its own, it may not be an accurate indicator that someone joined from an acquisition and may have been the CEO and founder but is now a VP of a department. Or someone may have went from a military role to a civilian role.

Implicit bias (unconscious bias) is a concept introduced in the twentieth-century workplace that recognizes implicit stereotypes through experiences and perceptions. One example that is used often by training companies is a blind interview for an orchestra where gender bias was prevalent. This profession is used as a stark realization of the origins of professions held by males. In a study done by the UCL Institute of Education at the University College London, they highlight the slow history for the representation of women in professional orchestras, citing the first female employed in a professional orchestra was not until the twentieth century. They use live simulation to illustrate the point. For this specific role, musical talent is the key attribute. This exercise is used to focus only on their talent without revealing gender or appearance. In the video, there is a curtain hiding the face of the candidate. They go so far as to eliminate the noise of high heels walking on the stage to further hide the gender of the professional performer. Gender, experience, location, and other factors play into this bias or preconceived idea.

I have had the opportunity to participate in two corporate training programs on this topic, and my current employer, in our corporate headquarters, has posters near the elevators on this topic encouraging people to consider different experiences for decision-making.

The different programs categorize the bias attributes into categories; I have seen categories ranging from three all the way to twelve or more. I found the training insightful and interesting. One of the newer ideas called out in the bias training is focused on location. Most companies are moving fast and want to make decisions and move on. When making decisions, looking for consensus, and creating work groups, many times leaders seek out people with similar experiences and common physical locations or time zones. This approach brings speed to the conclusion yet fails to recognize the opportunity for diversity which can be as simple as including someone with unique experience or someone from a remote geography. One of the great opportunities of the 2020 workplace, and the flexibility for many to work from anywhere, is opening new connections or broader collaboration.

This topic continues to expand in popular media as well as the workplace. I have seen other schools of thought where they do not buy into the "unconscious" part of the bias equation; I have witnessed some bold and candid comments about this in the context of gender treatment. I share this research with you because people are human and make decisions based on conscious and unconscious experience. It is important to recognize and have self- and situational awareness.

Although a simple introduction seems basic and innocent, now that I have shared this context with you, I encourage you to think differently as you set up introductions because they set perceptions.

The guidance here is to consider your audience. What will people tune out or tune into? Turn off autopilot, grab the yoke, and make an acceleration of spin. In the next chapters, we will break down "insightful introductions," providing a simple framework with real-life examples to model and incorporate within your workplace and community for positive and productive connection.

Trade
tricks
for
trust.

3

NO MORE TRICKS—
ASSUME POSITIVE INTENT

Failure is a trickster with a keen sense
of irony and cunning. It takes great
delight in tripping one when success
is almost within reach.

Napoleon Hill

I enjoy conversation,
I was not built for small talk.

TheGoodvibe.co

In many of my executive and team coaching sessions, I am often introduced as the provider of "tips and tricks," a phrase people use often to learn new skills, fast-to-market skills, fast wins, sharing, best of the best, etc. For me, both words are a catch-all for categories that should be spelled out. "Tips," to me, signals observations and shared learning. "Tricks," on the other hand, does not speak to me. "Tricks," to me, indicates you are trying to get something over someone else. "Intent" is a word I ground on, and positive intent is my grounding principle. Teaching someone a "trick" — in the context of how to attract, connect, and enter a business or personal relationship — is counterintuitive to me. If you want to make the statement memorable, and want the word to start with the letter "T," consider changing "tricks" to "techniques," "tools," or "teachings."

We have a dog that we love dearly: Ruby, a ruby-colored Cavalier King Charles spaniel. She is a trained therapy dog going through twenty-two weeks of training. Teaching her obedience, patience, and tricks has been a rewarding experience. When she does a trick, it shows her talent and creativity. This is how I would like the world to think of tricks.

Or think of a fascinating magician, such as the 2018 winner of *America's Got Talent*, Shim Lim, who calls himself a "sleight-of-hand artist." He is a talented close-up magic illusionist. Or consider the creative fundraising social media challenges to do a trick shot into a soccer net, or other tricks that demonstrate skill and creativity. I am sharing these examples because I am one to love tricks when they demonstrate spirit and innovation, but when used as a shortcut or getting around someone, I am challenged.

Words matter. You need to give strong consideration as a leader to how you introduce topics to the group, team, and/or customer. Taking the time to intentionally set the mood/stage/theme will give you a more likely opportunity to connect with your audience and establish immediate rapport. Often referred to as "presence," the way you show up includes your tone, energy, and language. Emotional intelligence and self-awareness are often used to relate your presence and ability to make human connections, or are leveraged to relate to the topic of the group you are communicating with. Another connection point is articulating what you intend to learn as part of the introduction. In this application, clarity wins over gimmicks.

Consider leveraging this thoughtfulness, planning, and intentionality in everyday interactions, not just on stage. Many people are often looking for the quick fix, not wanting to take the time to learn and go through the process's steps. There are countless references from world-class coaches and business leaders on process and mindset; both go together to create sustainable results. In the book, *High Performance Habits*, the world's leading performance coach, Brendon Burchard, outlines his reactions to his Ultimate Influence Model (UIM). He shares his research on high performers around the world, sharing the sentiment that people around high performers do not feel manipulated. "They feel trusted, respected, and inspired." He paints a graphic picture of the exchange of short-term success, built on characteristics of manipulation, and the long-term effects. I align fully with his call-to-action on how we will inspire the next generation of leaders' actions by emulating the interconnected model that highlights how to think, how to contribute, and how to model these attributes.

Bring *energy* that propels the workplace from routine to *remarkable*.

For me, in this context, "tricks" are quick fixes that are unsustainable. I encourage you to focus on the process, which includes the journey and experience, not just the end result.

Trade tricks for trust.

When reflecting on what we want people to remember about us or how we want to be introduced, my gut response is, "I want people to come away feeling better than when they entered the conversation." I want them to know I am interested in them and care about our time together. The word "present" is often used to explain this feeling. Easy to say, but hard to do when we have over thirty-five thousand decisions our brain makes daily on everything from driving to breathing.

The T word you need to consider is "tone." When you are introducing a topic, consider the tone and importance you are looking to gain, and how you intend to connect with the listeners. As a leader, you need to keep an eye out for the lack of creativity that shows up as routine. In many cases, you are having others put together content for you. As the purpose-driven leader, keeping an eye out for these simple opportunities to make improvements will deepen the connection, increase the energy, and set the tone for learning and listening.

My formal foundation on this topic was introduced to me in my first professional business program out of college: the Dale Carnegie Leadership Program. His teachings on first impressions focus on the other person and how you interact. These hundred-year-old principles have withstood the test of time and are highly relevant in our world today.

Mr. Carnegie breaks his "rules" down into a simple list of six topics. These focused areas have been the foundation of my personal and business life.

"The Six Rules" are:

1. **Be genuinely interested.** Be sincere, honest, and truthful when engaging with another person or topic, even when your mind is going another direction. This first one sounds simple, but in a fast-moving world where people are onto their next thought or the means to an end, truly taking the time to focus and be interested in others' point of view requires discipline and focus, while not making judgement.

   I have instilled this philosophy in my family. When checking in at a hotel, flight, or restaurant, ask the customer service agent their name, repeat their name, and look them in the eye. I remember the transformation of my husband when he saw how this mutual-success approach works well and both parties walk away satisfied. I cannot count the times we have witnessed people yelling at a service worker to get out of their way. Threatening to escalate, they may get their wish at the time, but the universe will not support this behavior; you get what you give. For the moment, you will get your way, but if you believe in what you give is what you get, you will win for the short term—however, in the long run, you will be left behind. Trying to understand other perspectives, experiences, and the parameters they have for their roles is important to learn.

Acceptance and empathy have a place in both personal and professional scenarios.

2. **Smile.** You can smile with your mouth, eyes, and your personality. Supermodel, TV personality, guest lecturer, and author Tyra Banks said, "On *America's Top Model*, I've always told my girls to *smile with their eyes*. We call it 'smizing.'"

   "Smizing" is a real thing. In 2020, amid the COVID-19 pandemic, people began wearing masks and learning to smile with their eyes. A smile costs you nothing and is simple. It can express words without speaking. In the song, "When You Say Nothing at All," Allison Krauss and Union Station share the statement that you do not have to say anything, that the smile on your face tells a person how you feel.

   One of the simplest forms of feedback that has stood the test of time in business is a smile. A smile can demonstrate that you acknowledge a person and are listening. A renounced psychotherapist, Dr. Amy Morin, breaks this idea down in her book, *13 Things Mentally Strong People Don't Do*, by stating the importance of "connecting the intention to the action. Acting 'as if' is a common prescription in psychotherapy. It's based on the idea that if you behave like the person you want to become, you'll become that. In reality, if you want to feel happier, do what happy people do—smile."

3. **Use their name.** One of Dale Carnegie's biggest lessons was a module around remembering people's

names. I embraced and mastered the module, which has served me well in business and social settings. It is simple and requires focus and listening. The idea is to truly hear and say the person's name and create a facial or word association. To the listener, their name is the most important word. Consistent use of their name in conversation increases attention and focus.

In the modern workplace, there has been discussion of the use of pronouns and personal identification. Using someone's name eliminates that guessing or misuse of gender pronouns.

4. **Listen.** Much can be said about listening. Passive, combative, and active listening are newer concepts and considered high-demand soft skills in the modern workplace. Truly listening involves feedback through verbal and nonverbal communication with a focus on attitude, attention, and adjustment.

5. **Talk in their terms of interest.** The weather (unless something remarkable), traffic, temperature of the room, or the basics ("I am a father of four . . ." or "I am a mother of two . . .")—these are all cool, but tell us more. It is interesting to see, in doing research on this topic, some of the top-selling books on the market offer advice on connecting many and are titled with connecting, networking, or communication. My perspective on that advice is, the conversation will feel comfortable from the start, but does not make for a deep connection, and if there are others observing the interaction who desire deeper connection, they

may avoid interaction. I support planning by doing research that could be a topic of interest for the person or the company. For instance, current events that are not polarizing. If you are going to share the weather, the traffic, or other routine areas, make a point to say why you felt compelled to talk about a routine subject.

6. **Make them feel important.** When Mr. Carnegie highlighted this bullet, he emphasized the importance of respect, reverence, and attention. In addition to the aforementioned focused areas, especially listening, I would add "recognition" as an intentional way to make people feel important. Taking it a step further to elevate their importance, thoughtful and purposeful planning and execution to recognize their success or intellect in a public forum or to a person's senior leadership can go a long way to elevate the spirits and talent of the person or team you are recognizing. Going two or three levels up can establish dialogue.

Many people do not feel comfortable doing this because of the additional attention. In my experience, this is not accurate, and most people in senior leadership crave feedback, especially from their staff, and many people are apprehensive to do it. The top excuse is "I do not know them," but highlighting specific behaviors and how they made you feel is humble and helpful.

In addition to Dale Carnegie's list of six rules, I am

adding another element of conversation: **small talk.** In the spirit of being unexpected, ditch the small talk. Small talk is used to gather information and get you comfortable with speaking to another person, but it is expected and people will only respond with politeness and no real connection.

I was invited to a women's leadership luncheon, and we started the introductions with everyone being polite and professional. When it got to me, I started with a story about my family and how we have a rule: "No small talk." That comment opened the floodgates for commentary and sharing and love. There was a pause in the conversation, as you do not know if everyone feels the same way you do about this idea. Then one of the women agreed and said, "Yes, 'big talk' only." The group laughed, the body language relaxed, and the formal façade retreated to open the door for authentic sharing. The idea of "big talk," a.k.a. "big ideas," resonated and deepened our conversation.

Time is well spent on a smile, a thank-you, and recognition. This is the energy that will propel our workplace and communities from routine to remarkable.

The following quote from Dale Carnegie's book, *How to Win Friends and Influence People*, summarizes his list that he created over one hundred years ago:

> "It costs nothing but creates much. It enriches those who receive, without impoverishing those who give. It happens in a flash and the memory of it sometimes lasts forever. None are so rich they can get along without it and none

so poor but are richer for its benefits. It creates happiness in the home, fosters goodwill in a business, and is the countersign of friends. It is rest to the weary, daylight to the discouraged, sunshine to the sad, and nature's best antidote for trouble. Yet it cannot be bought, begged, borrowed or stolen, for it is something that is no earthly good to anyone 'til it is given away. And if in the hurly-burly bustle of today's business world, some of the people you meet should be too tired to give you a smile, may we ask you to leave one of yours? For nobody needs a smile so much as those who have none left to give."

It is interesting he mentions "the bustle of the business world" years ago, which leads me to believe that, in the next hundred years, we will continue to be busy and pre-occupied. Taking the time to "leave a smile" will continue to build a society of those who care for each other.

Every second counts if you are trying to *convey a message.*

4

WORDS MATTER—
ESTABLISHING CREDIBILITY

Words are free. It's how you
use them that may cost you.

— Unknown

One kind word can change someone's entire day.

— Unknown

We are going to discuss three areas you can use to add dimension to your introduction, credibility, shared values, and insight. We will discuss the strategy to influence, inspire, and align.

As stated in the quote above, "Words are free. It's how you use them." Credibility is an area many struggle with because we want to remain humble. Intentional communication is important for working in teams, especially time-sensitive projects. An initial exchange of information can provide insight on experience and relationships that may be valuable or give authority and power to make decisions. For those in a selling capacity, incorporating an insightful introduction can uncover budget ownership or resources, such as talent and experience. It can uncover alignment to key projects or corporate objectives which may accelerate the decision process. On the flip side, credible introductions can uncover inexperience; often, people are not forthcoming with their influence and resource ownership. Aligning with credibility may offer experience that may reduce or identify risk in time, budget, and resources.

The credibility tenet plays out well for newly formed groups or meetings with external parties. A humble starter before introducing yourself or the team is a simple thank-you: "Thanks for inviting me." This plays out well when you are in a situation with multiple people and you are establishing alignment, power, and support.

As discussed previously, most of the time you hear people state their title, which, in most cases, does not create a connection or interest. The purpose of stating your title is to share your authority level, tenure, span of control, and area of expertise. As a listener, this offers a glimpse into the ego or power level of the person making the introduction. In observation, the most innovative leaders tend to say, "I look after XYZ," or "I have the privilege of XYZ." Because their title is on their business card or social media profile, there is no need to boast or share information that is not relatable to the audience.

A humble way to establish credibility is to share something that illustrates your commitment, scope, value, and authority. Instead of saying, "I am the lead project manager," you could say, "I have worked on solar-transformation programs for the last three years. On my last project, we patented the technology, and I am responsible for the team that will be creating this new technology with you. With my past experience in government contracting, I am sensitive to the importance of staying on schedule and compliance."

In this example, the leader introduced him or herself using an example of a similar project of scope and scale, and shared a successful outcome, as well as the value they would bring to the project by respecting deadlines and compliance. This extra information is helpful to the listener and will create a connection. This part of the conversation is an opportunity area to indicate your past experience working with this company, team, or group. There is an opportunity for interjecting positive outcomes or credible facts specific to the situation. This information is helpful in a buyer-seller model or a learning model where the listener is trying to gain insight of the presenter's credentials for the purpose of establishing initial rapport and trust.

Ironically, I was recently on a webinar hosted by a business university, an entrepreneur association, and a local business newspaper about writing a book. The sponsors/underwriters of the program were highly accomplished female leaders, but they spent their introductory time on their names and titles when they could have used the opportunity to say something about their favorite book, the courage authors have to accomplish their goals, or something personal about themselves. I find that many times academic, tech, or nonprofit event planners give a script, and the presenters do not want to challenge or deviate. That is where the unexpected comes into the picture.

Two experiences come to mind.

My friend was part of a technology association pitch contest for start-up funding where the speakers were all CEOs or founders. The format was something along the lines of name, title, company, what innovation you provide, market opportunity, investment opportunity, and value proposition. There were ten companies, with breaks in between each, going three at a time back-to-back. They had ten minutes or less to pitch.

On her drive to the session, my friend called me for some last-minute motivation. I shared with her that she would be one of many, with over a thousand people in the audience, and to change it up a bit. After a few minutes of convincing, she was in. This simple yet unexpected order of thought, along with her strong presence and compelling pitch, took home the title. Every other speaker started with, "Hi, I am Sue Smith, CEO of Company ABC. Today I am here to talk about XYZ."

Instead, my friend started with compelling facts about the challenges of the global disease affecting thousands of women, paused, and then said, "I am ____, and we are ____." People remembered her company name as well as her personal name because she started with the "why," then the "who," then moved to the "how."

In my career, I have had the opportunity to be the master of ceremonies, or introducer, of award winners. Often, these programs miss the balance of credibility and connection of the speaker with the audience, which is overshadowed by commercial endorsements. In the past, marketing teams paid for multiple mentions during a speech or the awards ceremony. This trend has changed to be more creative, such as sponsoring the scoreboard or having the cups the announcers drink out of sport the advertiser's logo. I often use the analogy of car-racing advertising, where your logo is everywhere. In sports marketing, the car and the driver have every free space considered as ad space.

In my experience in the professional and nonprofit world, where you are trying to make that personal connection with the audience and cause, the "pay to play" approach can be perceived as ingenuine. It is great that you or your company are supporting the activity or cause financially and with resources, but that is not enough. The personal connection and impact need to be shared, which is simple to do and shows empathy and connection. To accomplish this connection, the participants and leaders need to truly understand the mission and be comfortable making suggestions to the marketing and event teams and taking risks by "going off script" for a minute.

Many marketers or agents have their speaker say the company name multiple times, thinking that will create interest and credibility. In my experience from watching audiences' body language, they are tuned out to what speakers are saying because the narrative is about the company, not the audience.

Taking this a step further, when grouped with similar companies, they all seem to blend together. I have attended over one thousand business and nonprofit awards ceremonies, galas, and events where there is a speaking component that includes recognition. Typically, there are multiple presenters from different sponsoring companies. Regardless of the industry, the company tag lines all seem to blend together.

The speakers that are the most memorable are the ones that connect or affiliate with the topic or cause, not the ones that state their corporate name and a canned statement from their website that sounds like they are reading a corporate brochure. Think about it. The best commercials on TV are often the ones that tell a story and flash the company name at the end. This is a fine balance and requires knowledge of the group and situation.

A personal example is a school auction gala, where the wine is flowing, and there's great conversation and spirited bidding on the silent auction items. The organizer gets on the microphone and shushes the audience—yes, he or she says, "Shhhhhhh!"—and they close the bar to introduce you to the architect that designed the new school building. Then there is a presentation on all of the sponsors of the event, and on to a long thank-you of all of the volunteers who put on the event. After twenty minutes of this break in the mood, the program moves into live-fundraising mode with continued mentions of the sponsors.

If you have been there, you are more than happy to give the money so you can get back to the fun you were having with your group. The question I ask is, could you and your guests recall the name of the speaker or three of the sponsors? The answer is most likely no because you were tuned out. Although you were there to support the organization, the abrupt break in the flow of the program to repeated dialogue around sponsors caused you to tune out.

I have observed this similar situation in business and industry programs, and we can do better. It requires creativity, flexibility, and knowledge of your audience and venue. It is a delicate balance with conformity, time management, risk-taking, and tradition. Many people are stuck in the way they have always done things, which, in this situation, does not stand the test of time because of the introduction of enhanced digital, virtual, and additional elements. As shared previously, the attention span of a human is now eight seconds. Every second counts if you are trying to convey a message.

My most memorable introduction was when our team was presenting the top diversity award for a Nashville professional association. The event took place at a famous concert venue with an audience of seven hundred people. We were instructed to say our name, a description of what our company does, and then announce the award winner. There were nineteen different presenters for the different award categories, ranging from executive of the year to team of the year in different categories of projects. In addition, there were service-related awards for students, mentoring, and diversity. The production of this particular event was impressive—full sound, video that included clips of the winners, graphics, clear teleprompters, dramatic stage lights, music, and graphics that indicated the name of the presenters and company they represented. In short, the works.

You will have a new lens and knowledge for *better connections* and *results.*

And to top it off, did I mention the actual award was a custom guitar with our company's logo on it?

The instructions to the sponsors were to say their company name, what they do, and then announce the winner. Sounds simple, but when you have nineteen people presenting, it all starts to sound the same. Typically, these groups get event companies to coordinate the speakers and do not put much thought into the creative aspect. They are focused on the execution of the deadlines. I have found that as long as you are staying to the same timeframe, they are okay with personalized modifications.

For this example, we had to send our scripts in ahead of time so they could review the timing and have it loaded in the teleprompter. I shared with the organizer my desire to engage the audience and not be a walking billboard for my company, and she was open to the idea. Public facing script/copy is a fine line, especially for publicly traded companies. Many marketing teams overcorrect on this aspect to avoid risk for saying something incorrect.

My guidance here is, as long as you are sharing your personal affinity or connection, you are fine. If sharing a quote, give credit to the author. If legal and messaging are valid concerns, instead of sharing your stockholders' statement, the cover of your website, or standard business description, consider double-clicking on your corporate content social purpose, company values, diversity, inclusion, and equity statements. These are all interesting areas that may represent your culture and external messaging. Many times, there is a disconnect of the request from the presenter; they are not creative marketers, so they pass on the request for a company description paragraph, not considering the opportunity for customization. Most often, they pass on the direct instructions (directly forward contract or email) without understanding the audience and potential strategy opportunities for added differentiation and customization.

For this specific event, 100 percent of the other sponsors used content from their websites, and by the tenth presenter, they all seemed to be the same: detailing how they help customers achieve XYZ by leveraging ABC. Lots of tech buzzwords. They talked about how many employees they had, how many countries they did business in, and a list of their products and services.

Most of the speakers were not familiar with using the teleprompter or presenting in this large venue; that was apparent when they were reading their company description, as you could tell they were just reading it with no passion or interest. They started out excited when introducing themselves or stating how long they had been involved with the group, but when it came to the "required reading," you could hear the drop in their voices and the disinterest. You could see the attention of the audience shift to them looking at their phones or talking to their tablemates.

Rather than using this formula of the other twenty introducers, I started with an impact statement that related to the topic of diversity, and how diversity and inclusion are deep in our company values. I then called out the value adjectives for impact, pausing dramatically after each word.

Similar to "Thanks for inviting me," I added, "With the

privilege of giving away the diversity award," and then went on to add a quote from a famous musician related to the venue, setting that up by acknowledging and respecting the host location: "I can't think of a better place to be than Music City. Music is known as the universal language, knowing no boundaries of bias. As the great Jimi Hendrix said, 'To change the world, you must first change your mind.'" Then reiterating the host location, validating the leadership of the collective group, not just our company, I continued, "We are excited to celebrate these top leaders leading the charge in making Nashville one of the most diverse and inclusive places to work."

When we concluded, there was a line of high-fives on our way back to our seats. The impact of us changing the game changed others. The last speaker they had made the largest investment. The last speaker, with the teleprompter rolling with the long description of their role, talked about how large the team was, how long they had been serving the community, the top industries they support, and on and on. It was basically the front page of their website. The speaker looked around and said, "Heck with this . . ." and shared why they were involved with the group.

My team is now in our sixth year presenting this award, and I have noticed others have adopted this new approach of ditching the website description for a more personal statement of what their company has learned from participating in the ceremony, or what their company values and why this is special to them, or just ditching the pitch completely and celebrating the award.

Be unexpected.

Another way to test the uniqueness and memorability of your messaging to a reader and listener, especially in a public forum, is a simple exercise. You take your video, statement, or advertisement, and replace your company name with your competitor's name, and vice versa—put your company's name in place of your competitor's. If you are in an industry audience, event, or situation where one company is going one after another, or if you have a goal to differentiate your messaging, this exercise will highlight the fact that everything starts to sound the same and all the company descriptions tend to blend together. This is especially true when you are in an environment with many distractions. Every interaction counts; you can choose to go the polite, unmemorable route, or you can be unexpected.

In addition, learn to make interactions memorable and enduring by making the introduction your own by infusing your personality, your affinity, your interest, your passion, your curiosity, your discovery, or your connection into the presentation. As an example, at this same event, one of the presenters shared that they personally have been involved for the last ten years, and as a result of meeting all of these companies, they are relocating one thousand jobs to the Nashville area. Demonstrating you are part of the community or sharing your personal affinity to the group is especially important in situations where there is an investment (you are paying money to participate) to be at the event, meeting, or conference. You should be seen for your credibility, not your willingness to "pay to play."

I encourage you to observe this dynamic in the workplace, at home, and in your community. There are opportunities to see this play out, from the grade-school science fair to the many online and television programs where contestants "pitch" their product or idea to a team of judges in a fast-paced sequence. Notice those who start with the big idea, how they will help, what problem they are trying to solve, and who it will benefit. Starting with a bang is what is recommended. Starting with your name—"Hello, I am X, and today I will be talking to you about Y,"—is fine and polite, but it is not memorable.

I share these examples with you for observation of attention, energy, and where applicable, the results of new relationships or positive outcomes. The intentional planning and small change to the sequence will gain more attention and support. If you are able to lead and coach others, I recommend trying this out by having them practice the pitch with different sequences, observing their confidence and the connection to the audience.

And next time you are invited to that gala or awards ceremony, you will have a new lens and knowledge for better connections and results.

Be Open
to new
experiences
& the
unknown?

5

REVERSE CONVENTIONAL WISDOM

When you're used to being prepared to reject conventional wisdom, it leaves you open to learn more.

— Mayim Bialik

I n the spirit of addressing the premise of resetting routines, corporate B2B sales is a great profession to observe: The stakes are high, and the expectations to perform and add value are apparent from the view of the customer and employer. The last few years, I have had the opportunity to work with and learn from a diverse set of external consultants. It is an interesting story of how we were introduced that foreshadowed our relationship.

I was in Detroit for a CIO women's executive conference and was meeting the account team member for dinner to plan for the session. At the bar, he was with Curtis Brooks, principal of The Magis Group, and shared he was joining us for dinner. I tried all of my questioning techniques to uncover how they knew each other and the point of the meeting. Neither of them even said what company he was from or the context of his attendance for dinner. What cracked the surface and got them to break their act was when I shifted the conversation to food, and it turned out both Curtis and my colleague are big foodies. I then pulled out my phone and showed them my daughter's food blog. Curtis, having a daughter that also appreciated creating great food and trying recipes, was drawn in. They finally cracked, sharing their longstanding professional and personal relationship and the purpose of meeting me being to bring Curtis and his fresh ideas on "how to approach the executive" conversation into our company.

During our dinner, we found many aligned personal and business values, such as positive intent, love of learning, and challenging conventional thinking, a.k.a. breaking the routine. What I learned from bringing in a third party, although we aligned with the values, was we truly thought differently about many of the topics we presented on the onset. We often talk about diversity of thinking and trying new things. My personal experience has been that these are great words to say, but the majority of people tend to lean toward the known and what was effective in the past.

I describe Curtis Brooks as a catalyst for change, collaborating on modern thinking and breaking conventional wisdom. Through practice and experience, I came to see the shared value with the client and account team. The initial discussions with any new team were to give me the template, the letter, the email, the proposal, etc., to copy. What I learned from working with Curtis is that processes can be repeatable, the foundation needs to be laid, and the sender must have intentionality in what they produce. The bespoke approach is more work, but it is more effective.

Curtis uses many principles in his consulting business based on research and inspiration from thought leaders. The first one that resonates is a reverse on a popular question used in many sales training programs utilized to draw out what the prospect or customer's most pressing business problems are with the idea that you will be able to eliminate that pain. The word "pain" is often used in sales programs to find areas of improvement and focus.

Thus, the question: "What keeps you up at night?" I used to like this question, but now it has become so expected and routine and—to add further to the blurring of lines of work and home—it could cross into personal territory.

I recently read a large spread article in a major business newspaper about the priorities and stressors for cybersecurity professionals. The top question the reporter asked was, "What keeps you up at night?" To me, this is like asking an obvious question to a military leader, emergency room doctor, or even a caretaker. This question is especially dull when asked to leaders that run twenty-four-seven operations and are up at night serving customers, saving lives, or running their operations.

With the global pandemic in 2020, there was a shift from in-person conferences and meetings to virtual. The shift to virtual offered opportunity for access to broader thought leadership and collaboration. One of the popular delivery methods was an increased number of public-facing webinars with world-class leaders sharing how they are thinking about the change in culture, investments, and go-to market strategies to address the changing consumer behaviors as well as protecting employees and customers during this big cultural and transformational shift to the business climate. Many of these sessions were from the homes of the executives rather than highly produced sessions which allowed for deeper personalization, humanization, and engagement. When you see a Fortune 100 exec in their child's bedroom, or the garage or shed, wearing work-out gear versus an entourage in a fancy venue, the façade of their fancy office goes away and you are left on equal ground.

I saw this play out with a panel of global software company CEOs. When the talk got to a Q&A, the first question asked was, "What keeps you up at night?" I was encouraged; all answered the question on what they were hopeful for, what they had learned from the experience, and where they were focusing their time and energy for the future. These highly skilled, optimistic, and forward-thinking innovators had confidence to answer the negative question with a hopeful answer.

As a positive person, I have enjoyed using surprise and spin this popular question by showing a visual of the before and after. To change this paradigm and bring a positive spin, Curtis suggests the question "What gets you up in the morning?" illustrated with a bright sun rising over the city versus a dark room with an exhausted person twisting and turning.

"What gets you up in the morning?" signals a new day, a fresh start, optimism, and what could be. This new approach aligns with the emerging trend in the business world of sharing knowledge and positivity to balance the fast-moving digital transformation, global economy, and accelerated innovation.

In our coaching practice, we refer to conventional wisdom and routine business as the standard model. These traditional models align in discovering what problem needs to be solved with the obvious remedy being to relieve the pain, fix the broken, reduce expenses, and improve operations and productivity. This approach, on the surface, is reasonable.

A simple analogy is that I have a nail and you have a hammer—a perfect match. The introduction of this new idea about what brings you joy, purpose, and passion to get up in the morning is a modern way of thinking and opens the door for shared exploration and innovation. This approach has the potential to benefit both parties for a broader relationship expanding beyond the quick fix.

Bringing together the two ideas of what keeps you up at night and what gets you up in the morning has created a new approach to the traditional marketing funnel and sales pursuit plans or sequences, changing the traditional order of a B2B campaign. This is a topic whereon I have witnessed a huge variety of opinions and a divide of field sales and campaign marketing, where both have merit and value based on their point of view.

This is summed up by another counterintuitive statement. Russ Rausch, CEO and cofounder of Vision Pursue, focuses on awareness and learning to appreciate others' points of views: "The idea is to make it right, not to be right." This switch in approach plays out by flipping the conversation to the other and making it about them. The focus of the messaging is now around the idea of "inspiration versus influence," with the added attribute of *help* versus influence. Both approaches have their merits. If the intent is to help the person or company, the consideration should be to focus on inspiration.

Typical marketing campaigns have influence and market-creation themes. There is a shift to empathetic offerings that help or support the client or prospect. This fresh approach is showing up in high technology and manufacturing companies—along with healthcare—where you would expect this consideration. Examples of this are the P&G race-relations campaign, where they have candid interviews of mothers sharing the hard conversations they are having with their children, or the pharma companies showing stories of quality life experiences. Most surprising is the storytelling from the big oil and telecommunications companies, in which they show families and businesses in thriving situations with no direct mention of their product until the end.

A recent McKinsey article outlines guidance on new considerations for marketers, in addition to customer sentiment that they use the word "empathy" as well as "purpose."

Mindfully absorb the current moment.

With our work together, Curtis and I are finding in the current business climate that the most effective approaches to prospects and customers are behaviors and communications that articulate the desire to help. The context of influence, although not negative, has a focus of communication where you are trying to get someone to do something by talking about yourself.

Curtis Brooks has an exercise where he evaluates the company's messaging as well as their top-three competitors, and the results are a big surprise. The setup is, his firm does research on the competitors and creates messaging in the form of correspondence—digital or native—and it is shared with the group, presented as the best of the best of their peers in their company. The exercise continues reviewing all of the best practices—pointed out by the audience— then the surprise element happens. It turns out the messaging was not original, but a competitor's! This exercise is a great icebreaker to tee up deeper conversations and work around effective messaging, executive messaging, persona-based messaging, written engagement, drip campaign methodologies, differentiation, competition, and human responsiveness as potential ideas.

Here are four elements of the exercise we leveraged in our work together that brings a high level of engagement and new thought from the audience:

1. Expert marketers are experienced with the concept of a drip campaign, where a series of messages are provided to gain attention. The concept is not to say

everything at one time for the fear of losing the interest of the listener. With the exception of marketers, this method is not taught to sales professionals in a context with which they can relate. Time after time, we are the receivers of lengthy emails and direct messages from social media platforms that discuss how they know us, why we should call them, and if they can get fifteen minutes of our time, all problems in the world will be solved. As regular receivers of this type of communication, you would think we would learn not to be the one sharing so much at one time, as it overwhelms the listener. However, many times, we are excited about the new information corporate may have provided to assist us in our efforts to attract new customers and provide enhanced solutions to our existing customer base. Instead of holding back, asking questions, or getting to know the person first, we go all in and dump our information at once.

For instance, back in the 1980s when I was a fitness instructor, after returning from a weekend workshop, I was excited to share all of the new health knowledge and fitness routines with my class. Instead of sharing one or two new ideas, I would change everything and do a data dump of my learnings. The audience reaction was that they were interested but overwhelmed, with the ultimate result being them shutting out the new ideas and requesting our old routines.

Personal examples are good to draw out of your team. You need to check yourself to make sure you are not oversharing too many ideas at one sitting, session, or meeting. When you have the best new idea or method but overshare too much at one time, the natural reaction of most listeners is to tune it out. My husband, who toiled many years in the telecom and data networking industry, would often tell me when I was excitingly sharing lots of information: "Whoa, whoa. A lot of what you're telling me is being tagged 'discard eligible'"—an old 1980s frame relay congestion management reference. Data overload is what it is called today. The learning with this example is "go slow to go fast," too much is overwhelming, drowning, and excessive.

2. Curtis and I used a visual example to demonstrate the drip campaign for a large group of sales professionals. The visual of drip relates to water. As a setup, we elicited a planted volunteer from the audience. We had a watering can filled with water, a plant that can be held in the palm of a hand, and a large trash can to collect the water. To conduct the roleplay, we explained each part of the process and what each item represented. We asked the audience to picture the plant as the person you are trying to communicate with, and the water as the information you are sharing. I held the plant while the volunteer did the watering and Curtis did the narrating.

This simple roleplay really gets the attention of the audience, breaking up the use of slides or other media. The narrative explains that as you are sharing information, think about how your listener is consuming the information. We start the demonstration slow, and to cause a surprise effect, we dump the entire can of water on the plant, causing the water to go everywhere. Then expect an audience reaction and leverage that for further commentary or small group discussion.

I do a lot of coaching on digital platforms, and one area I see the most improvement in is this topic of saying too much at one time. From personal experience, I get hundreds of notes explaining why they like me, how they know me, problems they have seen, how they will solve those problems, and asking if they can get fifteen to twenty minutes of my time using their online calendar. This is too much at once. One hundred percent of the time, I mute these types of requests.

Please coach your teams on being simple. These steps are professional, but all together in one note, they are too much at once. Similar to my personal example of wanting to share all of my new knowledge with my class all at once, it was too much information at one time. Information overload can occur during the discovery phase of professional relationships. If the team is skilled in the art of asking questions, the exchange to inspire new ideas, information exchange, and exploration of possibilities are all great outcomes. Careful consideration to pace, volume, and attention span are elements of emotional intelligence, a.k.a. self-awareness observations to consider. Emotional intelligence is defined as the ability to understand, use, and manage your own emotions in positive ways to relieve stress, communicate effectively, empathize with others, overcome challenges, and defuse conflict. In business, there are adoptions of these concepts to test emotional intelligence with a series of situational questions establishing an emotional quotient, or EQ, as is often stated in coaching conversations when referring to self-awareness, emotional control, and actions.

For the most part, all the questions people are asking are reasonable and professional. The consideration should be around the sequence, volume, and timing. Often, some sales leaders or people put pressure on themselves to perform or get results in a certain period of time, which can lead to skipping steps or trying to do too much at one time, which, in most cases, does not have an optimal result. Effective communication of expectations, testing of content, and sharing best practices can all lead to more optimal return.

3. What pronouns (we, you, I, etc.) are you leveraging? They all have meaning and psychological implications in the receptivity to the message. I

found numerous articles on this topic of pronouns with correlation to leadership. *The Harvard Business Review* article states, "If you want to be the boss, say 'we' not 'I.'" It mentions several examples of world leaders ranging from King Henry II to Prime Minister Margret Thatcher. A recent speech provides a detailed example of the intentional use of pronouns to signal connection and influence. I saw this show up in the daily news when the mainstream media evaluated the transcript of a powerful speech entitled "Go Home" made by the mayor of Atlanta. The focus was on how she switched pronouns during her speech to start with a personal example and move into collective action. "[Keisha Lance] Bottoms had leaned on two pronouns, 'I' and then 'you.' As her speech wound down, she added a third. 'We are better than this,' she said. 'We're better than this as a city, we are better than this as a country.'" I share these examples as consideration to leaders when you are looking to get the buy-in and commitment of your team or community.

In the exercises Curtis and I did with the teams, we observed an overuse of the word "we" and the name of the company. The intention is to reverse the attention to the listener rather than talking about yourself.

Here is an example to illustrate this narrative. "At *Company X*, we assist businesses in creating financial wealth. *We* are the best at this practice because *Company X* has been serving customers like you for one hundred years. *We* value relationships. *We* are here to serve you." Although this narrative seems professional, what is really happening is the message is all about Company X, not about the listener. A simple tweak to the language referring to the name or the experience of the listener will make it more interesting to them.

Finally, to illustrate this point, remember back to a date you had when the person spent the whole time talking about themselves, not you. How did you respond? You may have been interested, but was the trust level or desire to learn more there? These are small details that can make a difference.

In most people's businesses, regardless of the industry, even a 2 to 3 percent increase in productivity can make a material impact on productivity and/or results. A simple, effective exercise is counting the "we's" in the communication, and then reframing the communication to utilize the focus on the receiver. This is a great exercise to do as a small group, live, or to have people send in examples of messaging prior to the session to share and critique. This is simple to do and very rewarding.

4. Lastly on this topic, there is heightened sensitivity on the use of gender-based pronouns. Consider leveraging names or subjects to mix up the writing

and make it about them, not you, if you really want to help.

Now I ask you the question: "What gets you up in the morning?" Consider this question with a different lens as your caretaker or family self, your business self, your community contributor self. Or, if you have reached a higher level of understanding of self, what are you grateful for, and what are you excited to experience or learn for the day? Or, are you mindful, absorbing the current moment? Are you open to new experiences and the unknown?

Whatever your world looks like, try something new. Surprise yourself. Be unexpected.

Experiencing
gratitude
opens yourself
to other's new
ideas and
thoughts.

6

SHARED VALUES

When we give cheerfully and accept gratefully,
everyone is blessed.

— Maya Angelou

People don't buy what you do;
they buy why you do it.
And what you do simply proves
what you believe.

— Simon Sinek

There is a strong interest in the self-improvement and business community around finding your "why."

A favorite quote I use often to ground people is "People don't buy what you do; they buy why you do it," from Simon Sinek. Social purpose is a new indicator of a company's solvency and values. This quote expands on a deeper purpose and the intrinsic value of the "why." The other positive trend in business is bringing your whole self to work, which shows up by expressing gratitude openly, sharing emotional topics—including health and family—and demonstrating empathy and humility.

This new purpose translates to the board or directors and C-suites of world-class, high-growth companies. There is a switch to focus from stockholders to customers and employees. This does not eliminate the need to make a profit; it switches the narrative to how they are helping rather than what they are getting. The human element is showing up.

An indicator that the sentiment is changing in modern business is a statement from a leading investment firm indicating they would only invest in companies with a flux of interviews with CEOs, community leaders, and CIOs on the importance of value alignment.

The Black Rock CEO, Larry Fink, outlines this correlation of prosperity in his quote, "Society is demanding that companies, both public and private, serve a *social purpose*. To prosper over time, every company must not only deliver financial performance, but also show how it makes a positive contribution to society." Purpose driven business shows up not only by giving funds to charities, but thoughtful, directed efforts for specific themes that align to the company's stated values and broader contribution to society.

For instance, if the company has a value to provide access to education, there should be a focused direction of funds, volunteer hours, and programs to this specific cause is an example of a social purpose focus. Some companies are drawn to social causes, such as ending human trafficking, food insecurity, and homelessness. Others may focus on education, bridging the digital divide, or health-focused organizations. Many are looking to solve local community-based causes, while larger corporations are putting forth valiant efforts to work with issues that affect climate change and the environment. The other area of social purpose that is showing up in the business world is inclusion, diversity, access, and equity for the companies' own employees, as well as the communities and customers they serve. Many of these areas used to be nice to have and the right thing to do, but at the end of the day, the focus was on the stockholders and the profits solely. The shift that is occurring is the recognition of the stability, innovation, and success for companies that can balance the focus of social purpose along with sustaining profits.

One of the positive aspects of the changing workforce is that people can bring their whole selves to work and incorporate their passions into their work lives. It is now acceptable to discuss areas of interest in a business setting. People find a deeper connection, interest, and energy level when they can express something that is important to them.

One of the three areas of making an insightful introduction is shared values. You can easily find what causes, interests, and passions people have outside their work life by doing research using people's digital footprint. A digital footprint is what they share and talk about online. This is a fast-moving market based on consumer preferences.

Examples that make up a current footprint in 2020 are: Twitter, LinkedIn, Facebook, online interviews replayed on Vimeo and YouTube, and earnings calls via transcripts Along with more creative fields like Instagram and TikTok, extensive business-focused research services, such as D&B Hoovers, Zoom Info, Inc., Boardroom Insiders, LinkedIn Navigator, Emissary.io, Delve Risk, and Databook, and with traditional analyst reports, 10K's, and web searches. Introducing a data point of interest found via research into a conversation needs to be genuine, not staged. I will share several examples that illustrates both sides to this equation of the giver and receiver of this advanced form of personalized research. This aspect is generational as Millennials and Gen Z have grown up with these platforms and tend to have a greater affinity in sharing information about themselves more openly and expect others to have had the opportunity to do that research.

Let's start with the disingenuous. I was part of a selection committee for a new CEO of a nonprofit organization and we had two days of interviews with final candidates from the search firm. One of the candidates, before their interview, said to committee members, "Hello, Bob. Great to see we both went to XYZ University," and "Hello, Sue. Great to see we both know Mary Stewart from ABC Consulting," then continued this greeting—our connection—for each person. The reactions were interesting: most of the committee thought this was great—he had done research—and were pleased with the approach. I felt differently because of the delivery of the information. I noticed when he was making these comments, his tone of voice and delivery were the same for every person. My impression was that he did not really care about the passion or relationship, but more about getting the fact attached to the right person.

Establishing credibility from a shared value requires intent and connection. Another example is when someone does research and finds they went to the same school, place of worship, hometown, etc. These facts on their own show potential shared values, but they are not foolproof. Just because you went to the same school or have the same hometown does not mean you have automatic trust and affinity with that person.

Many people gloss over this area and do not spend the time to learn and ask the right questions. If you are going to lead with this information, it warrants open-ended questions about the experience.

Looking a level deeper, clubs, sports, military, certifications, and other shared experiences are other areas to explore. Remember, nothing warrants immediate trust just because of your shared affinity. Exploring deeper personal, social, and community causes—including education and mentoring—are areas wherein you can get a 360-degree lens of the person to whom you are speaking. Authentically asking them to expand on why they are passionate about this work is an unexpected way to conduct business.

I love to observe positive reactions from individuals as a reaction to these approaches below. You can see the speaker lean in, open their body language, smile, and most importantly, leave their routine script. I call it "the energy and happiness meter." Taking it a step further, I love to observe the personal interactions unscripted; it can be a handshake, a reaction to a comment, a reaction to the experience. I notice familiarity, connection, closeness, and interest. It is enlightening and informative to make it a practice to observe others when looking at social media posts, watching live or recorded speeches, or even watching body language in virtual and in-person meetings. Three examples come to mind that illustrate this point.

I attended an executive alumni breakfast for the University of Georgia, Terry Business School. Ed Bastian, the CEO of Delta Airlines, was the panelist and speaker for the fifty-person audience. He was not an alumnus of the university, but one of his daughters was a graduate. (Note: My son completed the same program, which highlighted a shared experience and mutual connection we have as parents.) The talk was ninety minutes long and very business-focused. His company had recent litigation around unions and regulations, and he confidently and factually fielded all of the questions surrounding that. Near the end of Mr. Bastian's presentation, Ed discussed Tim Tebow, a Christian visionary he respected, and how he offered a session of his time with the top performers in the company quarterly. He continued to share his other passion of workforce development and the recent work he was personally involved with on a local economic development board.

The session ended, and there was a period allotted to get pictures with the speaker. As stated in my story with Heart, I do not usually recommend standing in line to meet the speaker. However, in this case I did meet him prior to the session, and I was planted in the energy seat, which I explain later in the book. The idea is a seat that is in the direct line of sight of the presenter where you are able to make eye contact and show interest (which fosters positive energy and confidence for the speaker whom you are providing micro-feedback). Positive energy reenforces to the speaker that their material is landing, they are being heard, and there is *interest*. When you are speaking to someone, the delivery is more natural than just reading a script and talking to a dark room or blank wall. In this scenario, I observed the entire presentation, noticing the positive and supportive connection between me and speaker, despite being in a large venue. Earlier in the session, I had met several people at our table, two of them were also waiting in the line to meet the CEO. Instead of looking at my phone or watch while waiting just to talk to the speaker, I got the people in line talking about the session.

It was almost my turn, and as I watched the people approach the speaker, they all said something about the company or themselves as their one-liner. Being proactive, I offered to take their pictures. When it was my turn, I mentioned our shared experience of being parents of students from the journalism school and mentioned my shared interest in the workforce-development project he was working on. His face lit up as he asked me to follow up.

The rest of the people standing nearby did not hear what I had discussed, but noticed the change in his demeanor and asked me, "How do you know Mr. X?" I shared I did not know him, that this was my first time meeting him, and they were blown away. "Well, it looked like he was talking to an old friend when he was speaking to you," they said.

And yes, I did follow up, and the CEO of this prestigious company sent me a personal note back.

/////////////////

My last example is from a common scenario to most high technology, pharmaceutical, manufacturing, or financial services companies that have outside sales teams. Gathering together for an annual sales conference is a rite of passage and a way to develop comradery and motivation in adding to the learning. The setting is a large ballroom in a luxury hotel in Las Vegas. Las Vegas takes people watching to another level, you will see Elvis impersonators in line, in full costume, at the grocery store, performers, tourists from around the world, and intermixed business conference attendees. I used this as an opportunity to observe the energy and attention of the participants of our session. I have seen moderators utilize noise meters to do a scientific measurement of the volume (crowd meters they use for sporting events, or to measure the level of applause). Instead of that instrumentation, we used our eyes and ears.

We witnessed this human experience firsthand, observing the energy, noise, and nonverbal communication of the audience during our session at a global sales conference for a high-technology company.

I was sharing this experience with my colleague, Rob Swymer, Tony Robbins Platinum Partner, trusted friend, and mentee, who has a growth mindset. Rob and I share the same passion for truly connecting with other people and to show up with love and gratitude. We often discuss the topic of being memorable and coaching teams to quickly uncover the shared values and passions of their audience.

In addition to the ideas for an insightful introduction of credibility and insight, we introduced the topic of shared purpose. When introducing yourself, one of the areas of opportunity to be unexpected is—rather than saying your name, title, and how long you have been with the company—you could ask, "What lights you up?" You can do this two ways: Ask this first, before getting into your own introduction, or you can add this as part of your introduction. An example of this prompt: "Great to meet you. I lead the professional services team and will be your executive contact for this new project. As much as I want to provide expertise to this project, what *light's me up* is seeing the impact we are making to improve the lives of these kids fighting cancer. I have dedicated my life to this cause."

To demonstrate the point that a deeper, personal connection *could* develop, we did three things to showcase the differences in research, sharing, and communication to bring the point home. The ideas we did are simple, but again break the protocol of the template we were provided as conference speakers.

The attendees had four consecutive days of meetings from eight a.m. to six p.m.. Sure, you have been there—as interesting and exciting as the content is, after two days, everything starts to blur together. Our intent was to create a sense of wanting to learn, more by changing the order to create variety and interest. The first idea was, instead of starting the presentation with our names, titles, and how long we had been with the company, we started with a quote and premise of why we were together. This is very effective as a grounding technique, setting the stage for what is to come and humanizing the speakers. Using the teachings outlined in the beginning of this chapter, we expanded on the "why" and shared examples of how people want to be around others who are excited, interested, and who care.

The second idea was to introduce each other, infusing our shared interests and why we care about them. This level of camaraderie was unexpected in this business setting; we even used the word "love." The back-and-forth, context, and element of surprise humanized the presentation/workshop. A more relatable example of this concept of introducing each other has been used for many, many years in the stand-up comedy world—remember going to a comedy club, the person introducing the next comic was a comic that already performed or would perform later. They're competing with each other yet also supporting each other and, in the case of the comedy club, their joint success helps the club, which means they'll get invited back. I mention this because others may realize this, and it may come across as a disingenuous "repurposing without recognition." Musicians probably do this as well—opening bands will announce and praise the band that is following them.

Lastly, with this human element as the backdrop, we allotted time for people to introduce themselves to the person next to them. We did this as a quick exercise, giving a start time and end time. We did this without sharing the best practices outlined in previous chapters about infusing credibility, insight, values, and "what lights you up."

We did a debrief with several people selected from the audience to report back to the broad group, and we found 100 percent of the responses were how long they had been at the company, where they lived, or their title. The audience was polite and attentive, all seated; the nonverbal action was a lot of head-nodding. To test out our premise of energy and interest, we repeated the exercise with a prompt this time, asking them to share "what lights them up" and explain what they are passion about.

Wow, did the energy and noise level in the room change noticeably! We were not sure what to expect, and the sharing went very deep, very fast. When asked to repeat the exercise to the broader group—"Stacey, tell me about Mark"—what people shared was incredible. They shared very raw, personal, and interesting facts. We repeated this exercise for three sessions with attendees from all over the world, and we experienced the same results: an increase in energy and attention and a noticeable yearning or interested focus to learn more. We observed this in the body language, facial expressions, and increased volume of the audience.

Now that we had the audience's attention, and some great grounding, we continued with another exercise to illustrate the point further. Rob and I did a roleplay of a peer-to-peer executive meeting where the team was validating next steps for the budget and conclusion of the agreement. Rob played the sales vice president who was the third-line manager for the sales team while I played the chief information officer who was the final decision-maker and budget holder. We did two roleplays with distinct differences in the approach.

Scenario one was very professional: complimenting the work the team had done together, laying out the steps and actions, and asking for support. The tone was professional and supportive. For the audience, they thought this was it and the modeling of a successful interaction to validate executive support and budget was complete. We had established peer-to-peer alignment, validated the next steps, and picked a date for completion. We could have left it like that, and for a sales conference, that would have been acceptable.

However, we took it to another level for people to consider the human connection and added shared values as an element in the conversation.

The second roleplay started, and the vice president mentioned he had seen the CIO's involvement with a mentoring nonprofit as well as a cycling nonprofit for disabled children. He shared his passion for cycling and asked how she got involved. What he did not do was say, "I see you like XYZ . . . I also like XYZ," and then move on, straight to business. That is not genuine. Instead, he showed genuine interest in why she was involved with these causes, and he shared a personal fact about a related experience.

The roleplay went on with this exchange of nonbusiness items, getting deep into a personal story of her military son who was part of Wounded Warriors. Both executives' verbal and nonverbal communications were telling of their connection by leaning forward, laughing, and making eye contact during the exchange. Then the executive did a time check and pivoted to the business topic, eliminating the long dissertation on how the teams are working together to an assumptive conclusion of the next steps for the conclusion of the agreement. The other executive talked through where she was going to be over the period of time and how she would personally make sure it got walked through their process. The meeting ended with her offering to walk them by the CFO office, where she would make a personal introduction.

This roleplay was inspired by a real-life customer inter-action. The team went on to say how incorporating shared values changed the dynamic for both parties. They shared how before they got the opportunity to send a thank-you/follow-up note, they were on the plane back and their inbox had one from the executive they had met. Before they even got the opportunity to send a thank-you/follow-up note to the executives with whom they had met, there was already one waiting for them in their inbox when they pulled out their laptops while flying home.

Being an actress in the roleplay, I will share that I was

invested in the conversation, especially when asked to explain my passion for the nonprofits and outside-of-work areas with which I was involved, I was so into it, the audience thought it was me. I played an active executive single mom with two sons, one who had recently served in the military and was just back home. Although I was acting, I could internalize the caring from Rob about causes that were deeply important to me and his shared involvement and passion.

Many times, we think we are alone in our thoughts, and this business interaction surprisingly validated the challenges my character in the roleplay was balancing in her life. This humanization and discussion of a business transaction assisted in illustrating to the audience that we are all people, regardless of our title and position of power. Empathy prevailed in this roleplay.

After this breakthrough of thinking and giving people permission to "show up" with their whole selves, we then had Rob introduce something very personal to the audience. He did a guided meditation/gratefulness exercise. It was so powerful and *unexpected*—not a normal agenda topic for the setting. When you offer something of personal importance, it shows vulnerability, interest, and trust, creating a human connection.

Both of us have continued to introduce mindfulness and mindset topics in the workplace, as well as being open to sharing and learning about "what lights people up"— getting to know the whole person and understanding their "why" so you can add to that shine.

Reset the routine of name, title, and tenure. Add this element of interest and inspiration to your conversations. "Sunday Best" by Surfaces is the song that speaks to this narrative of introducing gratitude to the workplace to bring your whole self to work. When you experience gratitude, you open yourself to new ideas and the thoughts of others — an important skill and an invaluable attribute for a mutually beneficial workplace.

So, next time you lead or participate in a meeting or introduction, remember to think about incorporating shared values. It is a great use of time if leveraged correctly and genuinely received.

Feel *heard,*
valued, and
energized

7

SEEK INSIGHTS

Insight enables you. Make sure you don't allow negative beliefs to get permanently set in your thinking, just the same way you wouldn't want fractured bones to be permanently set into place.

—— **Karen Salmansohn** ——

Lean into your curiosity about any issue, and there will likely be people to share a little bit more of their knowledge and insight and give you ideas on how to make change.

—— **Opal Tometi** ——

We all come to the table with biases and perceptions from experience. The oldest person in the room or on the call is not necessarily the most senior, and the person that talks the most may not be the most respected, etc. When entering into a larger conversation—in-person or in a virtual environment—rather than jumping right into the conversation as part of an insightful introduction, plan a question to understand others' knowledge or relationships.

It can be as simple as, "Who invited you to this meeting? What would success look like? What is your experience with XYZ? What is something that is not on your social media profile? What was your first job out of college, and what did you learn?" The point here is to remember this engaging conversation and convert your other interactions into memorable experiences, turn *off* autopilot, build the energy and human connection, and maximize the time.

In the '80s, there was a lot of research out of Xerox, GE, IBM, and other large companies on complex sales. Neil Rackham's fifty-year research on the art of selling has stood the test of time. In a Miller Heiman Group interview on their podcast, *Move the Deal*, George Moore talks with one of his protégés, Neil Rackham, who expresses his sentiment on the future of customer-centric sales. Rackham articulates his vision for an approach of starting with the customer and having strong alignment with sales and marketing. The following quote shares the ongoing, changing relationship and difference of perspective within sales and marketing that is important to recognize in order to navigate and collaborate on B2B (business to business commerce), not B2C (business to consumer), customer experiences. "In Rackham's view, marketing now handles the more transactional pieces of sales, opening up sales professionals to provide highly consultative expertise to their customers—a change he calls 'highly positive.'" Just the idea of being customer-centric, at the time, was a new idea.

In his book, *SPIN Selling,* Rackham shares a framework called SPIN, a form and sequence of open-ended questions, which is described as "SPIN = Situation, Problem, Implication, Need / Payoff." The idea is not to do the question linearly, but to add variety to your questions to really understand your customer or prospect. He encourages open-ended questions, which are questions that solicit a response. They typically start with "Why . . .?", "What . . .?", "How . . .?", or "Tell me . . ."

I was fortunate to have this training very early on in my career, and it has served me well in making human connections. The art of conversation and discovery is a critical "soft skill" in business as well as critical thinking. Rackham suggests you develop a *questioning mindset* to get people to think and reason, and to stimulate a two-way collaboration and discovery. He is known for introducing ideas that invoke thought, inspiration, and provocation in a professional way.

At the end of the podcast, the guest is asked, "What's your move?" This is the final quote offered as guidance to sales professionals or leaders they want to leave with listeners, and Mr. Rackham shares, "The first thing that you have to recognize is that selling today, certainly at the world-class level, is not at all about persuasion. It's about two things more than anything else: creativity and curiosity." This is an excellent quote that supports the premise that inspiration and seeking and sharing insight prevail over influence or persuasion.

This is easy to say but hard to do when people feel pressured to win or produce. The idea of "going slow to go fast" is something I instill in my teams and those I coach. Rackham goes on to say it is "more important to understand than to persuade." If you truly are trying to understand and seek questions and inputs to learn, you will develop a deeper connection and the opportunity to be a *catalyst* for creativity and change.

Another top 1980s author that is still popular today is self-help, business author Stephen Covey. His book has sold over twenty-five million copies, and his audiobook was the first US nonfiction book to sell one million copies. Covey outlines a person's "true north" and frames the conversation as seven habits. He encourages the method of "empathetic listening to genuinely understand a person, which compels them to reciprocate the listening and take an open mind to be influenced by you. This creates an atmosphere of caring and positive problem-solving."

As the chapter starts with seeking insights and leveraging curiosity, this idea is highly talked about in modern times when discussing the topic of emotional intelligence. I am noting that there is alignment to the fifth habit from *The Seven Habits of Highly Effective People* which says, "Seek first to understand, then to be understood." This supports thoughtful questioning *and* active listening. These interpersonal principals have stood the test of time and are relevant in the twenty-first-century workplace.

Mr. Covey used the Greek philosophy of *ethos, pathos,* and *logos* to start with your character (your intent), your relationships (the connection), and the logic of your presentation (your communication both verbal and non-verbal). He outlined and applied this method developed 2,300 years ago by Aristotle: "Ethos: Establishing personal credibility, integrity, and competency — character that inspires trust. Pathos: Listening with empathy; understanding others' feelings and points of view. Logos: Explaining with logic and reason; considering all known facts and perception." This approach supports the premise of entering into the interaction with positive intent, or seeking to understand rather than taking away or winning at the cost of others.

It is simple to say, "Seek to understand," but in the fast-paced, high-pressure, high-stakes world, those intentions are often overlooked. Like any habit, communication requires practice and knowledge of how to frame questions and sequence the interaction.

An article by Keith Rollag, PhD, and Jayne Mattson is an excellent summary to emphasize the points of seeking to understand and leading with empathy. They share and apply research in *Psychology Today* with their article "The Secret to First Impressions," which draws conclusions from Mattson's book, *You, You, Me, You: The Art of Talking to People, Networking and Building Relationships*, in which she suggests that the next time you introduce yourself — or get introduced — to someone new, remember four words: "YOU ... YOU ... ME ... YOU." After the initial handshake and name exchange, get other people talking about themselves (YOU ... YOU) by asking questions, showing interest, and following up with more questions to learn more about their background and interests. Then find an opportunity to share something about yourself (ME), and try to end the conversation with a renewed focus on them (YOU).

In other words, the best strategy for making a great first impression or opening a conversation or meeting is *not* by trying to impress other people with your own qualities and successes, but by ensuring they walk away from the conversation one, feeling heard, valued, and energized, and two, learning something positive and memorable about you.

In practice, I enjoy and am often frustrated by the lack of humility in how people ask questions. They appear to be complimentary to the person or group, but are really boasting about their intelligence and point of view. How often do we witness the person who gets the microphone and goes on to say their name, title—emphasizing the level—and then pontificates about their point of view before asking the question? Ask yourself, are they really asking a question, or did they just want their voice to be heard? What I mean by this statement is exactly as it sounds: did the person really have a question to ask? Or did they ask a question to learn something or clarify a point? Are they just taking the microphone to express their own point of view? It is a super-fine line if you are in a position of leadership and can coach others.

I encourage you to continue to observe and give feedback on this behavior. Bragging about success and stature may feel good in the moment, but it will not endure.

Seeking insights is another aspect to leverage as part of an insightful introduction, especially if you have a larger group or are trying to get the group to interact with each other in a collaborative manner. I have seen insightful introductions be incredibly successful when planned ahead of time and discussed with the team.

Some examples to include as part of the introduction:

- "Who invited you to this meeting?"
- "What are the top areas you want to cover?"
- "What is a successful outcome?"
- "What is your experience with X?"
- "What was the last successful project that you did?"

You may know the answers to these questions, but you are asking to highlight the insights to the rest of the group. These insightful questions can be a great bridge to the rest of the meeting and can identify power, relationships, and experience that is not evidenced by someone's title or tenure.

I have seen this be very impactful. As the people are sharing this information, if you are in-person, you can write on a whiteboard or flip chart. If virtual, take digital notes. This shows you are listening and offers the opportunity to connect comments to prioritize and refer to during and at the end of the session.

As shared time is precious, consider seeking insights as one of the three areas of credibility, shared values, and shared insights. Instead of the routine name, title, and tenue, you will connect faster, keep attention, and set the energy level of the interaction at a higher level.

Use your energy
to create
positivity and
connection.

8

THE FIRST APPROACH

A person's name is to him or her the sweetest
and most important sound in any language.

—Dale Carnegie—

I am now going to introduce the category of networking. Networking can mean different things to different people, and when you say that word, it typically results in a visceral response. This advice may feel uncomfortable or not standard to your workplace, but consider this: A great life example that most people can relate to is to visualize the first day—of school, meeting a new client or team at work, or being introduced to someone you want to meet personally and professionally. This can create mixed feelings of excitement, uneasiness, stress, warmth, and fear, with voices in your head going back and forth.

Reflecting on the two examples shared previously as part of the exercise with the large group in Vegas, one that was not prompted with any cues or topics, the second time a cue to share "what lights you up," by adding the prompt, it alerted the participants to go deeper, breaking polite routines.

Many factors go into the experience, including the environment, people around you, a warm or cold meeting, and your personality, which includes your physical and mental state, your tendency to lean toward introverted or extroverted, the list goes on and on. The number of books around this topic could fill a room!

Networking in business is classified as a "soft skill," one many people work hard to develop. Many high-tech, medical, and financial service fields focus their employee leadership and personal development training on the proficiency and discipline, and do not incorporate cross-functional twenty-first-century workplace skills. Many of corporate training programs that focus on communications, which include diversity and inclusion, and professional and selling skills, are now incorporating and prioritizing both soft and hard skills.

Soft skills that are important for a productive and harmonious workplace are communication, creativity, leadership, critical thinking, and teamwork. Hard skills are direct skills for the role, such as medical skills, math skills, and computer skills.

The point here is that networking is also a skill, and as such can be studied, practiced, and perfected.

///////////////////

I was once at a business conference in a room of eight hundred business leaders from the top car manufactures in the world when a local newscaster, with a big personality, did a quick icebreaker exercise. The setup seemed like we were going to have to "network" (get up and introduce ourselves to strangers). I could feel the hesitation from the participants. The moderator then asked everyone to write down what they did—not like networking—and it seemed like the next step would be to share with our seatmates. However, she surprised us by instructing everyone to crumble up the paper and throw it in the air.

The visual of eight hundred people throwing paper was spirited, childlike, and freeing. The room broke out in a murmur of expressions and laughing. Then the facilitator asked us to stand up, turn to the person behind us, and share what or who brought us to the conference today.

Her approach to getting the formality out of the way and relaxing the audience was effective. Similar to my experience of the group in Las Vegas, the energy in the room increased—not just the volume, but the genuine eye contact, leaning in, smiling, and closeness of the group. She then got the group settled before returning to her initial question about what they did not like about networking. Heads nodded in agreement as she told everyone that what she had asked them to do was actually not that bad, and they could do it *and* feel positive about the experience.

For me, networking is a topic I love to discuss and share perspectives on. When discussing with others, the tendency is to refer to a personal experience in the dating world. Some recall back to a time and place where the "networking" brought embarrassment or success, similar to the first day of school or a new job. The dating world or entrance into an organization is a great analogy to offer insights into those feelings of conquest, rejection, winning, and—the one that resonates with me—making a new connection that I would not have otherwise had the opportunity to encounter.

Pop television is another great place to find examples of how approaches and techniques play out. The American reality TV shows *The Bachelor* and *The Bachelorette* are overhyped and highly produced examples to use as a comparison. If used as a lighthearted roleplay, pop television highlights areas where we have emotion. The premise of the show is that the contestants are all vying for time with the star of the show. The idea is to strike up a conversation that makes the lead want to learn more about the person. It is not usually a good idea to mix dating and business interactions, but it is something people can personally relate to. There are reality shows similar to this on multiple networks globally, and they are referred to as "reality shows" with the keyword being "reality." Although overdramatized, they do illustrate the reality of life.

To further tie this example to real life, I have outlined the key areas often exemplified consistently. The other common design point from most of these programs is the *conquest*, or selection of a winner. Many professional sales executives, leaders, parents, and others unknowingly set up their teams, children, and individuals for failure by giving them that one-shot opportunity. Illustrated in the following paragraphs, all these scenarios are examples of a one-shot. I agree that first impressions matter very much, and so, in the outlined scenarios, these interactions are ways to engage and build rapport and trust. When a position of authority expects the employee, child, or individual to do an action and get something immediately in return, they are potentially setting them up for a quick win at the time, yet missing the opportunity for an enduring, trusted relationship.

1. **Do your research.** When asked if you have a question, a.k.a. your opening line, you shouldn't ask, "So, where are you from?" With access to bios and online content, it is easy to ascertain this information beforehand, allowing you to ask a more meaningful and memorable question.

    This happened to me recently in a business situation while doing a closing interview for a senior sales professional. After forty-five minutes of talking, I asked the candidate, based on the time, what was one question they had for me. They asked how long I had worked at my current employer. Really? That information is front and center on my professional social media profile. I gave them a second chance, and they had nothing.

Do your research so the questions you ask will be memorable and insightful to broker broader discovery and conversation.

2. **Practice name recognition.** Meeting people for the first time in a large group and remembering names is a skill that plays out in the show. As stated in the famous quote at the beginning of this chapter, a person's name is the most important sound to them. The first section of most of these TV shows is the initial meeting, where the lead is meeting a large group of people for the first time—similar to how people in business meet many others over the course of a week or month. Being memorable, repeating your name, pronouncing it, or connecting it to other words or phrases is helpful. The same holds true for their name. Repeat and use their name to create a halo effect. People love to hear their own name! Consider starting every other sentence with their name. If you are not sure how to pronounce it, then get that out of the way up front by asking them. Say it a few times to show you care.

3. **Be thoughtful.** Back to research. If you know the person has an affinity for something of mutual interest, bring it up or provide something of remembrance.

4. **Be authentic.** Be yourself. Connect with something

that you both value. This can be family, sports, nonprofit causes, etc.. The more personal you can get, the better.

5. **Do not trash your competition.** Many of the contestants spent their allotted time complaining about other contenders. This is *not* a good look. Rather than spending their time developing their own relationship, the contestant chooses to bad-mouth another person under the guise that they are trying to "protect" the Bachelor.

Likewise, in business, you get your five minutes with the executive or prospect, and if you spend it complaining about your competition, it will reflect poorly on you. I saw this play out at an executive Q&A. The CEO of the company took it upon himself to bash his competitor during his allotted fifteen-minute talk. It made him feel powerful, but the audience came away thinking that he was arrogant and self-centered.

Similarly, I often witness interview candidates who, rather than spending time on their experience and qualifications, speak negatively about their former employer or boss. This negativity shows unaccountability and leaves the listener wondering if they are a team member who places blame.

In a networking session, you have limited time, so use it wisely. This is not the time or place for trash-talking.

6. **Stay focused.** Stating the obvious here, but when in uncomfortable situations, people tend to over-indulge. Others see something for free and want to indulge or be part of the crowd. If something is important, go slow by having one or two drinks— or have none—until your business is completed. Oftentimes, the opportunity to network presents itself in a "cocktail hour" setting. Don't be the person who dives in first at the bar, forgetting this is semi-social, and semi-business event. Rather, consider nursing one drink—or have a "mocktail" (club soda with lime, etc.).

7. **Make friends.** Always try to make friends with those at the event. People like people who can get along well with others and have trusted relationships. Foster and spend time with others at the event, not just the main attraction.

8. **Go slow.** "Don't go in for the kiss or proposal on the first meeting." The ones that go in fast the first time may seem like they are getting what they want, but it does not last. If a long-term, trusting relationship is the goal, think twice. In a business situation, this is like asking for a raise, a sale, a partnership, in the first twenty minutes of an initial meeting. That may be your end goal, but if you go too fast and only focus on what you want rather than the relationship or what *they* want, you may win in the short term but lose credibility and trust in the long run.

9. **Dress for the situation.** Dress to get noticed in the right way. Consider the audience, venue, and how you want to portray yourself. "Dress for Success." Investigating the company culture, past events, or sessions will give you indication of how to *fit in* and *stand out* at the same time. Pay special attention to those in senior roles and dress to emulate them. A special color or something that ties into the theme of the session, event, or meeting can be effective. It is a fine balance to choose something memorable versus looking like you are in a uniform. A simple addition of accessories (for example, ties, scarves, pocket squares, pins, shoes, etc.) can be tasteful to make you memorable.

10. **Be positive.** People want to be around positive people who make them feel good about themselves. With limited time, you should focus on positive aspects instead of complaining about the venue, weather, traffic, food, or parking. That's not a good look.

On the show, there is always one or two people that spend 50 percent of their time complaining about the heat, how hard the chair is, how their feet are killing them, and other environmental aspects. Many continue to complain that they did not get 100 percent of their allotted time, going on and on about their dissatisfaction. A comparison in a work environment would be a job interview.

>Your interviewer is running late, and "your" time is now reduced. Do you start the interview with ten minutes of complaining, or do you plan accordingly?

I share this pop-reference analogy with you as a way to detach from the business setting and simulate one of the most popular "networking" environments, often a social setting that includes drinking. Even in this produced reality show, contestants later reflect on the true feelings developed from rejection, competition, discomfort, and treating others as a conquest or sport.

If you are truly networking, where you are seeking to build a community of interconnected people, manipulative aspects present a challenge. In business scenarios, people often use networking as a conquest and sport to win. When looked at that way, there may be challenges down the road for trust.

This passage from the letter of Saint Paul to the Philippians, 2:3–4, reinforces the importance of putting others' interests first: "Do nothing out of selfishness or out of vainglory; rather, humbly regard others as more important than yourselves, each looking out not for his own interests, but also for those of others."

The next time you are invited to a "networking" session, remember *The Bachelor* and imagine these scenarios. Focus on doing your research, being authentic, getting to know others, saying their names, and being memorable for your attention and interest, not for trashing the competition, complaining about the environment, or trying to get something. Enjoy the experience, be open to meeting new people, feel comfortable being uncomfortable, and use your energy to create positivity and connection.

Showing up is the *energy* and *focus* you radiate to the world.

9

SHOW UP

Presence is more than just being there.

— Malcolm Forbes —

The beginning is the most important
part of the work.

— Plato —

I interpret the concept of showing up to the energy and
focus you radiate to the world. There are many resources for this topic, often called "presence" or "brand,"
which speak to how you want to be perceived by others and
what energy or aura you want to create. In the spirit of *Be*

Unexpected, I am sharing some ideas and experiences that have served me and my teams well to create confidence and positive energy.

There are habits and motivators that set the stage for showing up. They can range from spiritual practices, mindfulness, and meditation to health motivators, to getting dressed, making your bed, and a variety of personal routines. This is an area of discussion that is personal and unique to every individual and how others relate to you. I will share with you elements that I have observed in the world of technology and nonprofit work.

Noting that her self-improvement techniques have scientific validity, I am a Dr. Amy Cuddy follower and reference her work often. She is a social psychologist, best-selling author, award-winning Harvard lecturer, and expert on the behavioral science of power, presence, and prejudice. Her TED Talk about power poses was actually the first TED Talk I ever watched, and it has stuck with me.

To help you along if you are not familiar with her work, picture the superhero character *Wonder Woman.* You see her with her feet planted firmly, equal distance to her shoulders, fists on her hips with her elbows making perfect angles, and eyes looking straight ahead. This is considered a *power pose,* as well as Amy Cuddy's signature pose. My takeaway is—whether there is proven evidence or otherwise—the act of planning intentional positive thought, distraction for the purpose of not worrying, and getting physical, Dr. Cuddy has coined the "Victory Pose" as a "ritual" to get you in the right mindset to perform. The

"Victory Pose" is simple: You stand with your feet hip-width apart in a strong stance, and then you lift both arms over your head in the shape of a V for "victory." This intentional "pregame" ritual works. It focuses on confidence by getting the blood circulating, increasing your height, and signaling that something great is going to happen.

You should explore others' pregame rituals, such as those of professional athletes or musicians, and develop your own. A lucky object, prayer, a breathing technique, music, a mantra—all of these create awareness and consistency.

Stu Heinecke ("Smoochin'" by Mark Knopfler), an author, marketer, and *Wall Street Journal* cartoonist, was introduced to me by Curtis Brooks, who was a guest on his podcast. Although Stu and I have not met in person, we have established a relationship of respect for each other's work through the phone and virtual communication. Stu has a unique and unexpected approach to meeting people. He outlines this in his book *How to Get a Meeting with Anyone*.

I broke this topic of how to have mutually beneficial, interpersonal engagement into simple steps centered around the questions where, when, what, who, and how.

1. **Where do you sit?** You should sit in the second or third row with your direct line of sight on the speaker. To figure that out, look to the podium, the chair where the speaker will be positioned, or the center of the stage. If you have the opportunity to meet or identify teammates or family of the speaker, sit with them.

I have had memorable and great connections made with the heads of public relations, corporate councils, executive assistants, and human resources. These are interesting people, and they will typically have different perspectives from the audience attending the event.

This advice applies to internal meetings, as well. The hardest group to present to is your peers, and you will find that if you follow this advice, pay attention, and offer a smile and show of interest, you connect and transfer that positivity to the speaker. If it is an event where the speaker has invited family members, this is a great opportunity to make them feel welcome and connect at a more personal level. After all, the speaker is going to be busy with the logistics of the speech or performance.

2. **When do you arrive?** Early. Arriving early gives you the opportunity to "read the room" and observe who is talking to whom. You will feel less stressed and avoid the annoyance of being late. Arriving early lets you witness the setup phase where you might meet people who, when the event starts, will be part of the formal program.

This is *not* the opportunity for you to be making phone calls or looking at emails. If you invested the time to be at an in-person session, than focus your attention there. If you do need to make a call or step out, go to an area that is not populated.

Otherwise, you may unintentionally signal that you are more important than the people at the session.

In my many years attending these business functions, I often coach teams to avoid "bee-hiving," which means clustering as one group. Instead, spread out and meet new people.

One skill I learned from sorority rush is called "the bump," a social cue on how to move from one group to another with a smooth transition. When you arrive early, you can observe the easy-to-talk-to people who can bridge a group of less-confident people. The art and act of making the introductions makes you warmer and approachable. The idea is to be part of creating a collaborative experience for all.

3. **What do you wear?** Something memorable. The point is to be an *individual*. The art of attraction and creating presences are interchanged in this example. If you are conscious of creating a presence, which is the art of intangible attraction, or being drawn to someone or something, then I encourage you to consider putting the same intention and thought into what you wear as you would when preparing for a meeting or any important interaction.

4. **Who do you talk to?** You should decide before-hand. Do some research and talk to as many people as possible. As aforementioned, try to avoid staying with a group of familiar people.

If I find myself in a group focused on small talk or going around the circle saying their names, titles, and what they want to get out of the meeting, I listen intently to their names, say them twice so I remember, and then move on to another group. I prefer not to discuss business or formal introductions, but rather go with the spirit of the day and see where it takes me.

5. **How do you open?** Relate the conversation to the shared event. In the example at the beginning of the chapter, when the facilitator prompted the audience during the exercise to share who invited them or why they were at the session, these are soft open-ended questions that are easy to respond to. I suggest steering clear of strong business questions. They may seem innocent—"How are our teams working together? Is there anything my team should be doing differently?"—but these are too much for a social setting. You will get a professional response, but the receiver will quickly move on. It is hard to be personal or casual when you open with this business focus. If you are there to celebrate or support an award or nonprofit, recognizing that fact— asking questions around that topic is light, thoughtful, and engaging.

I present an opportunity for you to stretch and try new ideas that may challenge workplace norms. Now is the time to disrupt and break the stale routines; life is too short. As shared in the discussion around networking, many of these ideas may seem unconventional, out of the norm, and uncomfortable, which is why you need to consider attempting and observing the energy and receptiveness of your listener.

To expand on the five aforementioned recommendations, I'd like to highlight four areas that most people consider *unexpected*. The first one is, if you want to meet a speaker— whether in office or elsewhere—the goal is to meet them *prior* to speaking. Waiting in line after the talk is not optimal unless it is paired with meeting them at the beginning, as well. Only meeting the speaker after the session can be risky because often, the speaker does their talk and is then ushered through the back entrance to depart. Then the master of ceremonies says, "Oh, sorry. Ms. XYZ gives her regrets. She had to leave for a flight to New York."

Of course, there are some opportunities where you pay to get a VIP experience. This setting is normally set up like the reception line after a speech. If you have this opportunity, leverage the insightful introduction principals and focus on the shared values aspect. Consider the line of people usually consists of a handshake, an offer of a business card, a compliment, and most people ask for something: an introduction, support, or direction. It may make you feel great that you got to shake their hand, but is the relationship enduring?

Moreover, think about how the speaker is feeling before their allotted time. There is going to be nervous energy, anticipation of the talk. However, if you follow the principle of meeting before they speak, you are showing interest and offering a "friend" in the audience. All performers and pre-senters want to connect with the audience. By this simple gesture of providing connection via your nonverbal communication—which includes focused eye contact, active listening demonstrated by taking notes or nodding in affirmation of key points, leaning in, open arms, sitting tall, and last but not least, smiling or showing emotion appropriate to the topic—you are showing interest, support, and empathy, which shows you are seeking to understand.

/////////////////

I am a student of life, and this topic of human interaction, to me, is foundational for inclusiveness, diversity, and equity. The science, cultural norms, societal norms, company norms, and emotional intelligence are all attributes that effect the interaction. In my leadership coaching practice, when I share these ideas often, I find that, within the audience, this is the first time in their professional career that someone has brought awareness to these aspects of interpersonal communication. To illustrate the topic of where to sit further, I share a few research examples in psychology, culture, and hierarchy that illustrate the complex intricacies when planning deeper engagement. *The Science of People* shares the work of environmental psychologist Robert Sommer, who was actually the first to find that where we sit in a meeting greatly affects several things:

- People's perceptions of you: How do you mark your territory?
- Your feelings toward others and what is being said in the meeting: Do you feel included or excluded?
- The status of your relationships

The science makes sense when having one-on-one conversations. Do you sit across from the person behind a desk, or side by side at a table? These are all well-researched, and I have seen them play out in real life. In fact, when I can influence the setup of a room, I prefer a horseshoe formation so everyone can see each other.

I recall taking a class during my master's program at John's Hopkins called Power. We learned about verbal and nonverbal gestures, physical stances, eye contact, and hand motions. There was extensive scientific research on the topic of environment, space, and human performance kicked off over forty years ago by Robert Sommer, an internationally known environmental psychologist. *The Today Show* even hosted a segment on this topic and interviewed modern researchers. This type of research is also used for negotiations and intelligence. Janine Driver, who heads the Body Language Institute in Alexandria, Virginia, has extensive research and training on this topic. She shares a few tidbits of her research that applies to classroom and common business scenarios. She advises that to "seal a deal, sit to someone's—like your boss'—left. That may seem counterintuitive, but it works.'"

My takeaway is that this matters and awareness is important. I am often in scenarios with classroom-style seating. So, where do you sit? In the front row? No. From my experience, for large venues, you sit toward the middle in the second or third row. The idea is you want to be in the direct line of sight of the speaker. The front rows are not really in the direct line of sight; they are under their chin. Now, the catch is, you need to provide positive attention and energy. Think of the invisible connection—a string or channel. You will provide calmness and positive feedback by this intention. You can take notes, but this will require you to put away your electronic devices and stay in the room for the entire session.

On the topic of being memorable, and what to wear, I had a podcast interview with Stu Heinecke—author of *How to Get a Meeting with Anyone* and an editorial cartoonist. Stu has a unique superpower where he combines his talents as a *Wall Street Journal* cartoonist and executive connector. Stu sends a canvas with a personal cartoon drawing and message to create conversation. This marketing outreach for his clients' using has turned this idea into a practice, named the "Father of Contact Marketing" by the American Marketing Association, where Stu turned his unique approach of inspiring a conversation into an engagement model. He brings his personality and act of surprise as a personal element, which creates a positive reaction where the receiver reacts by saying (or thinking) "Wow, who is this?" instead of "Who is this person?" We immediately connected; although our superpowers are unique to our skill sets, we had commonality in combining our personal interests into our interpersonal relationships that cross into the business world.

In the podcast, I shared my thoughtful approach of how to connect with and respect the organization and venue. I have had the opportunity to participate in professional color and stylist coaching sessions. They make the connection of what makes you look powerful, friendly, energetic, serious, etc. For me, it was a great interest—I have always loved fashion and looking "put together"—but not everyone is interested in outward appearance, thinking it takes too much work, time, or money, or they may prefer comfort over function. Depending on your environment, this may or may not resonate, but I share my observations because there will always be a point and time in your personal or professional life where this thought process will apply. As for me, I am fascinated by orators, interviewers, speakers, and such. I observe their words, gestures, diction, presence, and the reaction of the audience they are influencing, helping, and motivating.

I first observed the attraction and memorability of speakers during my fascination with White House press conferences, particularly how a petite woman with a red suit asked the most unexpected questions—Helen Amelia Thomas. She is best known for coining the phrase, "Thank you, Mr. President," after her questions, and was always noticed because of her consistency and professionalism.

Mrs. Thomas' fashion is a great example of what to wear. In a sea of blue and black suits, she always wore something that stood out.

My advice and affinity: theme dressing. What I mean by that is, you research the colors of the venue and wear those colors. Yes, I am serious. During my visit this year to Boston College, I wore maroon and gold, the school's colors. It was noticed. A simple icebreaker and it looked great in pictures. Another example is when I was in London, celebrating International Women's Day. I wore a St. John's purple suit. And yes, I had an orange suit for The Home Depot, red for Coca-Cola, a green jacket for Humana, and so on . . .

This practice dates back for centuries. For instance, the members of houses of worship have worn different colors to show affiliation for celebrations or observances. Examples are bright colors for the different festivals, white for most weddings (red in some cultures), and black for funerals.

You can consider using these external facets as a way to add connection to your audience or listener as we continue to expand into windows of people's personal lives. Bringing attention to something of common interest is a great way to connect and open a conversation.

This brings me to one of my most favorite topics: shoes.

One shoe can change your life.
━━━━━ Cinderella ━━━━━

Give a girl the right shoes and she can conquer the world.
━━━━━ Marilyn Monroe ━━━━━

Yes, I was the young girl who believed that great shoes — especially ones with sparkles — gave me special powers. When visiting my grandmother in Florida, I remember intently watching her put outfits together, and I was especially drawn to the shoes and jewelry. Playing "dress up" was a joy. My grandmother dressed for every occasion and lit up the room with her smile and personality. I wanted to be like that, and I reflected how at my mother's funeral, everyone made a point to say how "put together" my mother was and how hopeful she was to them by listening, teaching, and pushing them a little farther than they thought they could go. I was inspired by these examples of strong women and aspired to emulate their presence, poise, and power. These quotes summarized this content the best: "I make shoe contact before eye contact," "Good shoes take you good places," and "Shoes speak louder than words."

I was first introduced to luxury shoes by a great woman I met on a nonprofit board. She was one of the only women on the board. She likes to tell the story of how she looked me up and down, loved my shoes, and said, "I can tell we are going to be friends."

Early on when I was a sales leader at a fast-growing software company, every quarter the leadership would play a joke on the top performers. They would call and "punk" you, making up a story about something going wrong with your booking. For me, they always had a shoe-related prank. So, I got into the game. I made a point every quarter to buy one pair of expensive shoes, then I would hold them until our team made our goal. We made our revenue for eleven quarters straight (which equated to me keeping the luxury lavish designer shoes or boots as a personal reward), only missing one quarter by 2 percent. That quarter, I bought shearling, shaggy boots on clearance for thirty-two dollars. I am sharing this random story with you to illustrate how obsessed I am with shoes/boots and how they relate and tell a story to what was occurring in my life and those around me.

One of my most famous pairs is my tall, purple, suede, red-bottom, luxury boots. My team had just doubled in size and our quota was five times what it was the year prior. They were looking for significant year-to-year growth. I used this occasion to make a visual and memorable example by showing these crazy boots as an incentive for motivation for attainment of a far-reaching goal. At the time, my team was all male. I was able to connect the story with the boots to our growth. To this day, the past team members all remember that speech. Part of being memorable was the humility and a little self-deprecation that turned to humor as well as setting big goals beyond current experience.

This shoe experience is not just a female attraction. Most of the top designers are men, and they have men's lines, as well. Nice shoes are equivalent to a special watch, or dress or athletic shoes. They are a way to add flair and personality to your appearance. The utility, function, and fashion are all interesting in their own ways.

Dress shabbily and they remember the dress; dress impeccably and they remember the woman.

Coco Chanel

Dress how you want to be addressed.

Bianca Frazier

There are a few pieces of advice my daughter remembers, and this is one of them: It takes the same amount of time to put on a "wash the car" T-shirt as it does a dress shirt . . . so make an effort. It is not about the expense, whether it's from an off-price store or luxury designer, but how you carry yourself. Dressing for the part, dressing for the role, and making an effort can be simple and shows respect.

Keep your head, heels, and standards high.
━━━━━━━━━━ Lola Stark ━━━

I have found I can start a conversation with pretty much anyone about shoes, regardless of age, gender, economic status, etc. Thus, it helps me validate the investment in this wardrobe addition that is part art, part utility, and part personality.

For me, this connection is an indicator that the start of something great is going to occur. You may have other external triggers that set you up for that level of success. Self-awareness is key in understanding your emotional, chemical, and physical reactions. The mantra "play nervous," introduced to me by Russ Rausch, is a great visual for this idea. I use the pregame ritual example as a relatable example. What you eat, wear, the music you listen to, your prayers, your mantras get you going to achieve high success. For me, great shoes get me ready for what is next. It is not just the product itself, but the acquisition, selection, and feeling that is transferred to the experience.

> Anticipation, which is a mortar to desire the ability to imagine if as it's happening, to experience it as if it's happening, while nothing is happening and everything is happening at the same time.
>
> ━━━ **Esther Perel** ━━━

////////////////

Another way to connect with others in a personal way is to memorialize the moment. On Father's Day, my daughter's great friend visited for the weekend. She had her old-school disposable camera on hand and took candid pictures of us enjoying the lake. She got the film developed and used it to send out thank-you notes with a picture from that weekend.

I observed this memorializing practice in the business world from a longtime friend and mentor. I was on her professional association's board and attended many executive conferences with her. She shared four ideas that have served me well by making others happy and amplifying success.

One of her best sayings is "We are not here for the chicken dinner." That reference means we are not here to enjoy the typical plated food, but to really experience the company and the intended learning. In this way, she is big on meeting people, regardless of their position or stature. She has met world leaders, movie stars, politicians, CEOs, and in more cases than not, that first meeting is the start to a broader relationship. She has no agenda, just the authentic approach to meet new people. Her outlook is one to be admired and replicated.

My friend took the idea of memorialization of the moment to the next level. She would take pictures, frame them, and send them with a personal message. I have never done this but admire her approach.

What my friend does reminds me of the photographers you encounter in extremely tourist-y areas. The ones who coerce you into taking a picture with some novelty and then give you a receipt to pick up a framed version of that photo later that day. What I take away from these examples is the idea of taking pictures of a special moment and sharing it with the person, something that will be remembered as an act of gratitude.

Another idea for leveraging the power of the picture to highlight a relationship goes back to the first newspapers that featured society or community columns. I had always wanted to be in the paper, and my friend shared a preference of most newspapers. According to her, and validated with two local business columnists, newspapers prefer group pictures of three. To be noticed, you need to seek out the reporter early in the session to ensure that they find you at some point in the event to photograph you. Because you have made an effort to meet the reporter and create a relationship, you have a higher probability of making it into the newspaper they work for. This can be very simple yet effective for getting your name out to the business or nonprofit community.

Furthering the conversation on connection and credibility, another way to demonstrate your affinity and commitment to mutual success is to be on equal ground. If you are entering into a conversation or negotiation and want to establish credibility, embody the customer. You know the saying "The customer is always right." This fact came to light for me with two business situations. Both were "escalations," which translates as walking into situations where the customer is not happy or trying to leverage a negative experience for gain—usually financial.

In both scenarios, the customers were Fortune 100 retail companies, so that was easy. One was a large fashion retailer, the other a home-improvement store.

Scenario one: The client executive on my team was a platinum cardholder and had his account up on his device. I made a point to mention when I walked in the room that my outfit was recently purchased from one of their stores and that I had had a great shopping experience.

Scenario two: With the large home-improvement store, I mentioned I had just made a large home-improvement purchase and brought my receipt.

These door-openers quickly diffused the situations, demonstrating that the point of authority was not to yell louder to get more, but to collaborate for mutual success.

I encourage you to reset the routine and get creative in building affinity with the customers you serve or communities you support. When you can demonstrate you are thoughtful, invested, and want to be part of their world, both sides will benefit and the human connection will be made.

Lead with:

Listen

Open

Vulnerable

Engaged

10

FIND YOUR VOICE

Quiet people have the loudest minds.

━━━━━━ Stephen Hawking ━━━━━━

I enjoy speaking on "finding your voice." In fact, I enjoy it more than any other topic because I feel I am offering new light to a skill that will serve people in all aspects and enable them to be more effective contributors to their workplace and communities.

I had the opportunity to go through many formal leadership and coaching programs on finding your voice that informed my thoughts on the topic. Now I even find myself offering feedback upon first meeting people in all walks of life. I am in situations where very smart people who are in positions of influence are often muted or marginalized because of the tone or volume of their voice, the prefaces they use before their main points, or because they start off with an apology for no real reason.

This last point is the most common diminisher. In this fast-paced world, in the spirit of resetting routines, I have observed that many people tend to start off a conversation or meeting with an apology related to small talk, like traffic, the weather, technology—really anything nonsequential. Unfortunately, it does not create a positive energy or authority when you start a conversation or speech that way. If something important needs to be acknowledged, that is fine—recognize it and then move on. As leaders in business, I encourage you to observe and coach, and you may see a correlation with performance and attention to the speaker for those that start off with "I am sorry, but . . ." If you spend your time on unnecessary apologies, you have wasted precious time.

This observation continues with preface words that researchers call "diminishers" or "distractors." Starting sentences with, "This may sound crazy . . ." or "May I add . . ." distracts from the meat of your thought.

The confidence to speak up at the right time is a learned skill, and there are many factors that contribute. They range from skill, confidence, verbal and nonverbal communication, social norms, status, gender, age, and other factors. There are extensive resources that create awareness and action for this complicated topic.

To illustrate the reaction of the listener in a workshop

setting, I perform a simple exercise. The setup and materials needed are colored sticky notes (or a piece of paper ripped into two parts) and the song "You Say" by Lauren Daigle. I got this idea from Molly Fletcher, a sports agent turned keynote speaker and host of the podcast, *Become a Game Changer*, who utilized this technique of a physical expression for a value-setting exercise. She had each of the participants write down on five sticky notes the most important person, thing, or value they held. This could range from family to writing each of your children's names, God, health, faith, etc. One by one, she asked the participants to crumple up one and throw it away. The first one seemed easy, but when it was down to the last two or three, there was anguish. The goal of this specific exercise was to evaluate and reflect on the person, value, or idea that is written on the last paper standing. When you hold that paper in your hand, written in your handwriting, and are asked to reflect on your life and where you are providing your time, talent, and attention, it is powerful. For most, it was not only powerful but emotional, adding dimension and perspective to life's most important values.

I have replicated this exercise multiple times with teams I have led, and in every case, there was someone who was brought to tears because they realized they were not present with their family. As shared in the exercise around networking, the idea of the listener having the opportunity for individual reflection with the safety of not having to share with others—which creates vulnerability, or in some cases, privacy concerns—is a contributor to internalization and further thought, along with the physical act of writing the words down, crumbling the papers, and seeing them fly in the air.

For this specific exercise, I start with asking the audience to think about who or what has supported them and write that down. Then, on the other paper, write down who or what does *not* support them. Some examples are a grandparent, a boss, a sister, and an experience. I tell them to think hard about this answer, and that they will not have to share with anyone. I play music as they are thinking and have a visual of quotes and photos that illustrate this point.

Then I stop the music and do a dramatic countdown before asking them to physically crumple up the paper, because it does not serve them. Then I say, "One, two, three, throw!" The physical aspect of seeing others get rid of baggage and being part of a group is cathartic. When I do this exercise, I appoint someone to take a picture or video of the action. It is great to memorialize the thought. I then ask them to keep the positive things they've written down in a place of importance.

I introduce the topic of the feeling of belonging, collaborating, and recognition with this exercise for two reasons: One, it gets the group thinking introspectively, and two, it opens the mind to why the person may not feel worthy or have confidence to contribute.

The word "power" is often associated with being heard, and power in this context is authority, strength, might, and energy. The *Forbes* article "How to Convey Power with Your Voice" does a great job of summarizing the key points and extensive research on what your voice says about you, such as resonance, volume, speed, diction, and presence. Susan Adams, the article's author, shares many of the theories of Columbia University's Professor Adam Galinsky, who has spent the last fifteen years publishing 150 articles on leadership, power, and negotiations. The specific research she shares involves students listening to recorded speakers' voices and answering questions related to their credibility, status, and ultimately, their power.

Galinsky's conclusion from his study is, ". . . envisioning yourself in a position of power before you speak or head into an interview can greatly up your chances of coming off as powerful and confident. The easiest thing to do is, before you speak, think about a time in which you had power. That will have the affects you want to have without forcing you to have conscious control over your voice."

Many of these aspects we cannot change, as they are physical attributes, but some we can change or improve, if desired. It is interesting that one of the other examples and pieces of advice the *Forbes* reporter gave is the opportunity to observe and improve the tonality of your voice to gain respect and power. She offers an example of how Margret Thatcher leveraged a voice coach to improve her presence.

I, too, had the opportunity to experience speech therapy, which is different from speech coaching. Coaching focuses more on your presence when delivering a speech, how to connect with the audience, present the material in an engaging and non-distracting manner, and create emotion. For this example, I am speaking of speech language pathology

(SLP), which is taught by certified medical therapists. When I was in college, I worked at a health club and events company, teaching aerobics to groups of twenty to five hundred people, so I was yelling all the time. Soon, I developed vocal nodules, which are common with many singers. The choice was operation or speech therapy, so I chose the latter. It was a unique experience for me in the waiting room with anyone from young children with delayed speech to up-and-coming pro athletes who were learning to speak to the press. Granted, I received this speech training as part of a medical condition, yet looking back, I benefited from the exercises and observations to modify tone and breathing.

Now, we all cannot change our voices; they are part of our physical being. The learning point is awareness of yourself and others so you can facilitate collaborative conversation.

One of my most memorable experiences speaking was to a top university's women's alumnae group. Most there were about five years out of college. I posed the question, "Most of you were supported from the age of ten, knowing you were smart and would go to this university. You were told you were the best—and you are. You were recruited by the top company in the world with multiple job offers. Now, you are an employee. Are your options and ideas heard?" Sadly, the answer was no. So we discussed what could be distracting their voices from being heard. We did a quick audience experiment, and one woman asked a question with a long preamble and apology beforehand. Another woman asked a question in a tone of voice that most would consider meek or childlike. In a "safe space," we discussed the observations. I have yet to do a presentation where this scenario or setup, where a woman demonstrated one or more of these habits that distracts from their being heard, has not played out. This personal experience fuels my desire to educate, collaborate, and make change in the modern workplace. I will continue to be committed to changing this dynamic. I have found, 100 percent of the time, there is a highly qualified, intelligent woman who expresses challenges with not being heard or others constantly taking credit for her ideas or work.

In another talk at a top private company, I was invited by the SVP and CIO to their all-hands group. This was my first-time delivering content in a mixed gender setting. All the previous sessions were all-female and, in most cases, similar ages. This audience had variety of gender, race, sex and age. The preface of this talk was, "Are you a father? Are you a leader?" And the group all had one of those affiliations: a woman or underrepresented person, father or leader. It took courage and trust to discuss this simple yet vulnerable topic, since most businesspeople do not learn or talk about these attributes. One of the senior women from the back of the room raised her hand and said, "So, what do I say before I say something?" I looked at the executive and he said, "Just say it . . ." So simple and powerful. Saying you are sorry, "If I may interrupt," "May I share," "This may sound crazy," "I just want to add," diminishes the speaker's point. Lorrie Thomas Ross, the author of "I JUST Wish Women Would Stop Saying Just," passionately encourages women to take "just" out of their vocabulary. The consulting firm, Speakeasy Inc. of Atlanta, Georgia, refers to these words as "sugar coating."

It is interesting to observe people of authority as they speak. This is especially elevated on calls where you cannot see the participants—just hear their voices. It is interesting to observe how people transition and contribute their ideas and comments. You can observe that those with confidence or power will just jump in with their statement, and others will add these prefaces, such as "May I interrupt," "If I may add," or "Excuse me." I would like to suggest testing this on yourself as well as those who are part of your team, especially people you are working with or mentoring to get their ideas heard.

Lastly, using the word "just" to introduce topics of importance played out as expected at a women's executive session I was leading. I put the executive co-presenting with me on the spot to point out how she said "If I can just add . . ." before every sentence. In the setting, we were all women supporting each other. It was fine, but the point that was made was, if you are in a mixed-gender audience, with those with high power, how would they react to your points? The sentiment of the audience was to just say it; that is what the men do. In my experience, these subtle yet intentional behaviors make the communication situation a level playing field. This experience validated the plea from the executive and branding coach calling "just" an unnecessary word. And like other four-letter words, "just" can have a time and place to connect with audiences, show power, and demonstrate authority to emphasize a point.

Awareness, preparation, observation of the words we use, and reactions from the listeners are all opportunities for enhanced communication and connection.

Those with a voice that is not as deep and strong need to embrace their uniqueness and be aware of their words. Quiet voices are a great addition to the greater group. If we really want to embrace diversity, equity, and inclusion, we need to observe and consider these factors.

Leaders need to embrace their employees to make sure they are heard. That can be as simple as making sure the least confident and most quiet people talk at every call or meeting, and soliciting feedback and thoughts from the quiet ones.

A bird doesn't sing because it has an answer, it sings because it has a song. Each of the men and women that we honor today has a song.

— Maya Angelou

When I present the idea of making sure everyone in a meeting gets a chance to speak, I often get the discussion around politeness. I am from the Maryland/DC area and now call Georgia my home, and yes, in the South, people are polite. The idea is not to be rude, but to observe those with power and identify their diction and prefaces, and consider this as data inputs to the strategy.

Another consultant that I follow, and whose leadership classes I have taken, is Judith Humphrey. In her book *Taking the Stage*, she offers a great list of reminders to consider when connecting with your audience.

- **"Use real language to project authentic leadership. Choose words that are natural to you."** Back to the example I gave of giving an award and reading the company website description from a script—if the words do not feel natural, your audience will pick up on that, and this lack of authenticity can set the stage for judgement and mistrust.

- **"Be genuine. So many speakers fail to inspire their audiences because they speak in an artificial language. Avoid jargon."** I have worked in high technology my entire career, with parts of my career in vertical areas such as telecommunications, mobile communications, software, federal government, the energy sector, and the media sector, which all have a unique list of acronyms. Then you add the corporate- or sales-related acronyms, and then the project-management ones, and you have an alphabet soup! Here is an example for a sales conversation: "Our company is leading in the 5G digital ESP, and the ASAP project team is here to support your XVII program." This language is great for those in the room that are part of these teams and organizations, but outside of those specific groups, they may have different context. My favorite federal example is sharing two of the most popular acronyms used in conversation: CLIN (contact line item numbers found in government contracts) and CSC (civil service commission, card security code, computer science corporation, cyber security center, the list goes on). Those are used in many different applications and mean completely different things. In my coaching to clients, this is an easy fix, and most people do not realize that the three or four initials to shorten a complex idea make it easy to remember, but can have multiple applications depending on the listener's perspective. It is fine to use the jargon, but spelling it out so people do not have to ask, assume, or wonder will make your language clearer.

- "Eliminate 'filler.' Too many speakers fill their talks with unnecessary clutter—often to buy time while they're thinking. Expressions such as 'to be honest,' 'I have to admit that,' 'You know,' or 'Um . . .'" Many people do not think about these filler words. We are trained early on to avoid reflex-oriented words when we are thinking. Silence can be very effective; a dramatic pause or relaxed silence can bring the audience back to your thought and give them time to absorb what you are saying.

- "Show confidence. To show this confidence, be very sparing in your use of qualifiers such as 'I think,' 'I guess,' or 'Hopefully.' If you have to guess or you're just hoping, you're not a leader." This goes back to the advice of get your words out. Say it!

- "Be conversational. Use everyday language. For example, say 'but' rather than 'nevertheless.' Say 'to' instead of 'in order to.' Formal language can sound insincere." I suggest relating to the audience and utilizing local customs for the area or company you are interacting with, considering what country you are in, if English is the first or second language, and the age and authority of the listeners. A little research can go a long way to make this connection if done sincerely and openly. If you are not sure, you can preface the comment or use of the language and ask for feedback or reaction from the audience.

- "Be warm. Your language should convey your feelings—feelings of excitement, enthusiasm, pride, commitment, as well as concern and even disappointment." Amen to this one! I completely agree. When you can share your emotion and connect with the audience in a warm and authentic way, you are on the right track. This is an area where you can introduce vulnerability, humor, and even self-deprecation.

Make Space for Love in the Workplace

"We are here to love each other.
That is why you are alive.
That is what life is for."

Maya Angelou

> "Choose a job you love, and you will never have to work another day in your life."
>
> — Confucius

The words "joy" and "compassion" are front and center in workplace conversations and media interviews when leaders discuss their team, culture, and grounding leadership principles. These attributes are associated with the phrase "emotional culture." In the *Harvard Business Review* article, "Employees Who Feel Love Perform Better," the authors make the connection to culture and leadership. "First, broaden your definition of culture. Instead of focusing on 'cognitive culture'—values such as teamwork, results-orientation, or innovation—you might think about how you can cultivate and enrich emotional culture as well. Emotional culture can be based on love or other emotions, such as joy or pride." In Simon Sinek's breakthrough leadership book, *Leaders Eat Last,* he connects employees and customers to the success of the organization and people over profits. He uses the word "love" throughout his narrative.

> "Customers will never love a company until the employees love it first."
>
> — Simon Sinek

As a leader, you need to feel confident that you can empower and engage with others in a relationship built on trust and compassion. It is acceptable and appropriate to use the word "love." I have numerous personal examples about how saying the word out loud in a business context can be inspiring with the first example being a casual observation, when leaders receive public recognition or awards. They often start with "I love what I do," or "I love my team." These simple statements show humility and connection. One of our world's leading technology visionaries, as part of his legacy, quotes:

"The only way to do great work is to love what you do."
— **Steve Jobs** —

From a personal perspective, I know this is working when I find myself, time and time again, in conversations with colleagues whom I am coaching or collaborating with and the conversation ends with the words, "love you" or "love ya." Several times, the person was embarrassed they used those words and apologized . . . in that moment, they instinctively blurted out the word "love" as a reaction to feeling gratitude and being heard. Instead of letting it be an awkward moment, I leveraged it to discuss the feeling, recognizing the trust, respect, and gratitude. We shared how we would support each other in the future. These conversations are inspiring during times of success and celebration and excel during times of crisis and challenge.

Lead with LOVE: Listen, Open, Vulnerable, Engaged

To Lead with LOVE, consider these questions discussed in previous chapters.

- **Listen:** Are you listening to understand? Are you present? Are you considering their perspective?
- **Open:** Are you amenable to new ideas? Do you have welcoming body language (i.e. leaning in, eye contact, etc.)?
- **Vulnerable:** Are you guarded? Are you willing to get personal?
- **Engaged:** Are you Showing Up?

  - *Do you love your job?*
  - *Do you love what you do?*
  - *Do you love your company?*
  - *Do you love your team?*

These are important questions to discuss as they inform and build culture. In the modern workplace, culture and purpose surveys, rankings, and amplification are part of the attraction of talent, suppliers, investors, and customers. You will see culture mentioned on front pages of company websites and annual reports. Companies, public relations agencies, and individuals leverage global publications and news outlets such as *Forbes*, *Fast Company*, *Fortune*, and others work-related publications to benchmark and highlight their experience to peer companies. The trend of these "best of" lists are focused on popular attributes and affinities such as gender, age, geography, and is highlighted in the reports and awards. An example of this is "Best Place to Work for XYZ," "Top Influencer for ABC," etc.

In the *Harvard Business Review*, Duncan Coombe states, in his article entitled "Can You Really Power an Organization with Love," "If just about every person on the planet has at some point spoken about the centrality of love to well-being, why do we hear so little about it in the context of work?" He discusses actionable ways to show up with love even without saying the actual word. His work is citied in many articles on this evolving topic, highlighting generational differences and societal changes.

In doing further research on this topic, in the context of love, leadership, and the place for them in the modern workplace, I was encouraged to find roots in the idea from an early Martin Luther King Jr. sermon. Many societal ideas have been seeded at the community level and then are incorporated in the business world. His thoughtful approach to the topic is one to be admired and actioned. In the sermon, "Levels of Love," Dr. King reminds us of the connection and variety of the forms of love and how they can extend beyond individuals to impact society. He describes the lowest form: utilitarian love. "Here one loves another for his usefulness to him. The individual loves that person that he can use . . ." There are some people who never get beyond the level of utilitarian love.

This self-interested, egotistical use of people is often what shows up in the workplace. The type of love we want to evolve modern workplace thinking and action is what Dr. King calls "rise to agape . . . an all-inclusive love . . . Agape is higher than all of the things I have talked about. Why is it higher? Because it is unmotivated; it is spontaneous; it is overflowing; it seeks nothing in return. It is not motivated by some quality in the object. Utilitarian love is motivated by a quality in the object, namely the object's usefulness to him." To illustrate further on how these principles materialize in the modern workplace, consider a visual of a maturity model where agape is higher than utilitarian love. Here are some examples:

1. The leader of the team leverages their resources to bring together a collective decision that will result in prosperity for all involved, taking no credit as the leader but relinquishing to their team.
2. The leader leverages the influence of one of the team member's relationships to get what they need, they do not recognize the contribution and take the credit at the expense of their team.

Make it your mission to observe, practice, and reset the routine expectations to create a better experience for all.

Reset routines to be part of the world *without boundaries* and *bias.*

11

AUTHENTIC CONNECTIONS

If you want to go fast, go alone. If you want to go far, go with others.

African Proverb

The richest people in the world look for and build networks. Everyone else looks for work.

Robert Kiyosaki

Your network is your net worth.

Tim Sanders

My first real paycheck was an entrepreneurial endeavor with Avon. I invested in the "kit," attended the sales/leadership meetings, and committed to the process. I was fourteen. This was in the 1980s.

Before online selling was available, companies relied on direct sellers set up in a hierarchical structure often compared to "pyramid selling." You do well and then you recruit others under you, and then they recruit others, and so on.

My friends participated in healthcare, cooking, and other new-to-the-market direct sales products. Tupperware made a comeback in the '90s, and Amway was very successful. There was no Costco, so the idea of bulk cleaning supplies was genius. In the 2000s, so many friends that have highly successful cosmetics and jewelry businesses leveraged this model.

My husband and I still jest about our first two experiences being approached by our "network" in a nonoptimal setting. We were invited to our first couples' information session that was advertised as a fun cooking lesson, and we were excited to learn advanced cooking techniques and hang out with other couples. The demonstration was excellent, we learned how to make gourmet appetizers, the wine and beer were flowing, and conversation was engaging. Then an announcement happened: We were to stop, sit in a circle with clipboards and catalogs, and had to be a "captive" audience for a thirty-minute presentation on the "entrepreneur" business and why they do it. Sadly, I have seen this approach so many times, and I am *not* a fan.

The speaker started with a copy of a paycheck, sharing how much money they made from selling these products. Then they went on to share that this was a break from their family monotony and a way to meet people. What if every corporate business meeting opened like that, where the recipient shared what their personal gain would be for a positive interaction? Needless to say, it was a complete buzzkill. We excused ourselves, but did make a big order because we liked the products.

A similar experience happened when our friends—another couple from the health club we attended—invited us for a "presentation." Same thing, but with more pressure on investing in a business. When we politely declined, we never heard from them again. When every compliment and conversation leads to, "I want to sell you something to build my business," I will pass. It is a small, but important, difference when the person doing the selling truly believes in the product or service, has personal experience with the benefits, and articulates that passion for mutual success, then the model works. If the discussion is only focused on what the business owner will do with the profits, the discussion can come across as ingenuine. It is always a great opportunity to share how their support has contributed to your success and prosperity of your family and community, but leading with this conversation is not recommended. I implore all direct marketing companies that encourage the business owners/sellers to start their presentations with a copy of their commission check to focus on the benefits and personal experiences of the product and the services.

I love the idea of encouraging kids to be entrepreneurs with this direct sales model. It is a great way to build real-world experience, especially when building a résumé early in their career journey. What is challenging to me is often these companies are more interested in the family network of the seller than *developing* the skills and career of the seller. These opportunities are still great examples and career building with the suggestion and intentionality of entrepreneurship, community building, and value. As stated earlier, this is a great place to insert "trade tricks for trust." Now, in a world of personal privacy, protection, and opt-in laws, the engagement models have evolved. Which brings me to the professional network platform, LinkedIn. I joined this platform in 2006 as part of my management by objectives (MBO) with IBM Media/Telecommunications Software Group. Learning this platform, Twitter, and other social networks was part of our credibility in the market. LinkedIn was purchased by Microsoft in 2016, and in 2020, it has close to seven hundred million members globally. I have had the opportunity of experimenting with this platform and sharing best practices for representing a professional profile and protocol for building a network. It is a personal experience and preference. These networks will change over time. The current indication is that communities of interest are *thriving*.

I encourage you to consider these data points and commit to infuse one or two into your company, team, or relationships:

- Enter into the discussion to learn.
- Be passionate about your activity, your company, your team, yourself.
- Stay away from:

  o Entering into a relationship by stating how you will personally benefit from them.
  o Exploiting a friendship for personal gain.
Boasting on the number of connections, friends, prizes,

cash totals, sharing awards, and honors is great, but counting friendships as a way to build credibility is boastful. It is personal and a fine line.

An example most people can relate to is picking a real estate agent who is a top seller with demonstrated results on volume and revenue. Yet, I would not want to do business with an agent who focuses on how much income they made from a particular transaction or who they leveraged to get the deal done. I would be supportive if they shared that, because of my business, they could support their kid's college. The difference is humility and positive intent.

To encourage others to approach you or interact with positive intent with the principle of "together we are stronger," I recommend utilizing profile bio and description fields to highlight what you value, the teams you thrive on, what inspires you, and what you want to learn rather than what you will gain from the interaction.

In June 2020, a LinkedIn State of Sales US Edition study showed 88 percent of LinkedIn users said they are more likely to do business with a warm introduction. My first management role was managing a health club. One of the key metrics we used were referrals and, in the digital world, we can see global recommendations from the community. I bring up this point with simple personal examples, such as you would be more likely to choose a cleaning company, caretaker, or medical professional from someone in your "network." To me, a network is like the saying "It takes a village." The same principal applies for business. Collecting cards or contacts for personal gain may make you feel wanted and powerful for the moment, but if used in a manner that breaks trust, your legitimacy and sincerity will diminish.

The opportunity to leverage technology to *enhance* the art of conversation is evolving and opening new opportunities. A popular use for technologies is organizing communities of interest. These groups are organized and offered in many different options. One of the consistent features is "tagging" as a way to categorize, catalogue, and crowd source. I expect, moving forward, there will continue to be use of the hashtag function to organize communities of interest, target advertising, attract conversation strings. I highly recommend researching, testing, and planning your positive intent and interaction.

My favorite LinkedIn hashtags that show what I value are #leadershipmatters, #servantleadership, #gratitude, #mentorsmatter, #womanonboards, #womenintechnology, #nextgenerationleaders, #workforceofthefuture, and #collectiveimpact. Fun ones that I follow on social media have to do with shoes, gardening, or family: #willworkforshoes, #garden, and #familyfirst.

The new digital health-and-fitness applications and intelligent appliances, such as Peloton, have incorporated the hashtag to identify your "team" or interest. Hashtags like #onepeloton, #warriors, #pelotonmoms, and more are motivation, demographic, and affiliation–based.

For business, you can align with communities of interest to meet others virtually, exhibit thought leadership, and amplify a topic. I love this quote from an extraordinary teacher who envisioned a broader world, becoming the first civilian to be selected from a group of eleven thousand applicants to go to space on the *Challenger* spacecraft in 1986. She now has a legacy of hope and opportunity:

I have a vision of the world as a global village, a world without boundaries.

— Christa McAuliffe —

This book opened up with the idea of the walk-up song. Along the way, I leveraged music to connect my thoughts to my environment. I am sharing the song "If Today Was Your Last Day" by Nickelback to reset your routines to provide energy, connection, and liveliness to the modern workplace. I shared the examples in this book for you to consider how to create and foster a positive life experience. I shared ways to break the ice by being unexpected and humanize the grind of work so it does not feel like a rat race (where people are placed in a competitive struggle for power) but a race for humility, empathy, and community, where the sum of its pieces are greater than the success of an individual.

Imagine a world where you can get stuff done and make true connections that can change your life beyond the confinements of the workplace, as we are all human. Treat others like you want to be treated, and recognize that we can learn from everyone, regardless of position, tenure, or title. Reset the routines to be part of the world without boundaries and biases, sharing experiences with the human connection.

B -Bringing

E -Enunciation

To the Expected

B -Bringing

E -Empowerment

To the Expected

B -Bringing

E -Engagement

To the Expected

B -Bringing

E -Ethics

To the Expected

POSITIVITY CREATES LASTING EFFECTS

///////////////////// *EPILOGUE*
A LETTER FROM THE AUTHOR

What if you could enhance your relationships and make your work relationships more valued and connected? That would not be a bad thing, especially considering how many hours we spend at work, thinking about work, and actually performing work tasks. What if you could enter these formal settings and reduce drudgery and replace that with positive energy?

This book is meant to inspire business leaders to engage more in unexpected ways. Now you have had the opportunity to reflect and observe your actions, those you lead, and the business community. *You* are a part of what changes will be made to improve your life experience and those of others. Are you ready to make a change? As Lisa McLeod stated so eloquently in the Foreword, "What makes a person or event unforgettable? Why are some experiences so compelling, while others are just ho-hum?" Being unexpected is *the* key to standing out in a cluttered world. We can have a balance of respecting authority, social norms, and tradition while infusing fun, authenticity, and joy into any situation, serious or playful. Lisa continued with, "experiences become more memorable when they break an established pattern. When something (or someone) changes the frame, it disrupts our expectations. It is this very disruption that causes us to pay attention. Interestingly enough, you don't need to be extravagant, or even charismatic, to be unexpected. You simply need to break a pattern and step out of the usual ho-hum."

I give you permission to create the change you have within you to be the best version of yourself: original, vibrant, and fresh.

The quiet and clarity came from prayer:

You are the light of the world. A city set on a mountain cannot be hidden. Nor do they light a lamp and then put it under a bushel basket; it is set on a lampstand, where it gives light to all in the house. Just so, your light must shine before others, that they may see your good deeds and glorify your heavenly Father.

———— Matthew 5:13–16 (NABRE) ————

These words spoke to me, as if God were speaking directly to me. The feeling was overwhelming but was pushed aside as I got busy.

The chaos came from an exciting but somewhat predictable professional scenario:

Twenty Days of Travel

I had a big company trip to Las Vegas for a week, then an FBI symposium at Boston University, then off to London for International Women's Day. All the aspects discussed in this book were observed in real life as if it was a screenplay of the topics.

My company trip opened a door I did not expect: A colleague and I did a session that was very personal and mindful, not something normally done in this venue—a big risk. We were welcomed with open arms, tears of joy and release, and so many hugs and handshakes.

Then, in Boston, I used many of my coaching ideas with people I had not met prior, and in one hour, we became fast friends and had an incredible experience.

Then London. This experience was really cool as I had tested some of my material on an audience in London, but not a broad international audience before. It resonated with the audience as well as the other speakers.

Life Needs to Be Lived (Not "Life Is Short")

While in London, the COVID-19 global pandemic got serious, and my husband and I cut the trip short to return to Atlanta. Being accustomed to traveling 75 percent of the time and having evening sessions in addition to normal meetings, I found myself with a lot of extra time on my hands. Quarantining had me doing all of the fun creative projects, cooking, and working out, but I am goal-oriented. So, I made a goal to be published.

I had previously contributed to two book projects and several podcasts, but nothing on my own. I made a goal to publish three articles. I did two self-published and one as a contributing author, then I was hooked. After attending a webinar, with three out of the four authors in attendance being women I know and respect, they said, "You have to just do it." So, I did. I dedicated every weekend to writing with a goal of finishing by my birthday.

Forever—is composed of Nows.
══════════════ Emily Dickinson ══════════

My perspective is shaped by the life experience of losing my father, mother, and stepfather all to pancreatic and brain cancer in a three-year period. They were all sixty-one years old, at the pinnacles of their prospective careers. All were in great health (as it seemed) and had little time from diagnosis to death. Attending their funerals and meeting the lives of those touched via work, teaching, mentoring, and from afar touched my heart and motivated me to focus on what legacy I can leave rather than waiting until I am over the age of eighty to think about that plan.

I got my own wake-up call one week before my fiftieth birthday. Finally squeezing in my routine mammogram, I received a call the next day for a retest. I went out for a Friday happy-hour boat ride with my husband and, while relaxing, my phone blew up, sharing the news of the death of one of my early mentors, the chief information officer of a Fortune 100 company. He had just built a house on the lake and was planning his retirement. This news brought up thoughts of my mortality, something I was not ready to think about. That Monday my doctor called and told me that I had breast cancer. That is a story for another day when we can meet. I will tell you I learned so much about myself, the disease, and put *faith* over *fear*. I share this personal account because we often are our own worst critics and do not give ourselves permission to do something outside society's constraints or timelines. We need to focus on the now's, for they may pass. And those now's can be how we impact society for a positive life experience.

Thank you for reading. My intent is to inspire you to do one new thing or smile more during your day and live a life of gratitude. If you have the courage to bring this light and gratitude into your professional world, you can look forward to engaging in more unexpected ways to improve relationships and shape a bright future for generations to come.

I look forward to hearing and learning from you.

www.be-unexpected.com
marvabailer.com

///////////////////// *GUIDE*
BE UNEXPECTED IN
THE MODERN WORKPLACE

Insightful Introductions

Unexpected Insight: Faster connection with those in the meeting/session. Positive energy to fuel productive interaction.

Exercise:

Reframe Introductions: Walk-up Song

1. Have your team identify and demonstrate the following:

    a. Their walk-up song

        i. Ask them to select a song that illustrates who they are or what motivates them. The direction can be vague since the goal is to learn more about their personality and what they value. In this case, surprises are a good thing.

   ii. Select and offer commentary on the motivation using open-ended questions such as, "What were you imagining when you picked this song?" "What motivates you about this song?" or "What positive experience do you recall?"

   iii. Impressions: Ask for impressions from the other team members. Did they expect that song to match the personality of the selector? What surprised them? Did they relate? What feelings or memories did it create?

2. Long Meetings & Music

  a. Try for a team meeting that is three hours or longer. Reflect on the energy. I recommend, between breaks, have a DJ play music. It keeps the energy up, and when the music stops, it's a cue to get people's attention.

3. Insight, Credibility, Shared Values

  a. Have your team demonstrate the following: Set up a context for a roleplay. Let them know who they are speaking to by setting up the bio of the character. Are they an executive, what is their decision-making power or authority, and any other elements to make the scenario as real as possible. Have each member break into groups of two to four and simulate the three different areas: (1) Insight, (2) Credibility, (3) Shared values. Then, reverse the roleplay where they have to introduce the team or one of the team members using these categories. "Who or What Inspires You?"

4. Values Ice Breaker: Sticky-Note Exercise

a. Tee up the workshop of self-reflection in a "safe space" and give the participants sticky-notes and a pen or pencil. Ask, "Who told you that you could or could not do something?" "Who supported you and told you can do anything?" Let them know this is private and they will not be asked to share. Play music while participants are thinking about it. I recommend playing "You Say" by Lauren Daigle.

b. Next, have them crumple up the negative "voice" paper. Then, instruct everyone all at once to throw the paper to the middle of the room (or, if doing virtually, you can have a picture of a trash can, landfill, etc., as the visual and have them throw at the screen). Offer them to keep their positive paper and put it on a mirror, in their car, on their computer screen. Depending on the group, you can have them share their experiences. I have done it both ways, where it was all individual to small or large group sharing's.

c. *Reminder:* Have someone take a picture of the act of throwing the papers. This can be in-person or a screenshot of the virtual call. When you memorialize the activity, it brings back the experience. Can be shared as a culture amplification/multiplier in internal newsletters or on social channels as an example of personal development.

5. Advanced Planning Room Setup for Optimal Interaction:

   a. *Reflection:* I support the mantra "control the controllable," yet often many leaders defer key details that can change the energy and focus to others by not being specific with their requests. Many leaders make a request, "I need a room for a dinner for twenty-five people" or "I need a room for the day for two hundred people and three meals." I give great respect to those that do event planning as a profession.

   b. Similar to the suggestions about lighting and music for sessions, environmental, ambiance, and visual stimulation will change the energy, physical and mental. I personally will not do an all-day, in-person meeting without access to a window. Sometimes, this is not possible in large ballroom scenarios. In that case, I make sure to have access during breaks and meals. I recall a meeting in Chicago at a hotel on Magnificent Mile. The main group was in the basement for our all-hands sessions. I made a point to indicate my desire to have a room with windows (and was the only one accommodated because I made a big deal out of it!) It does make a difference. I follow this same approach when planning team or customer dinners with larger groups, having access to external space for relaxed conversations. I am sharing areas of opportunity to stand out and be memorable as well as foster deeper conversations. All take thought, pre-planning, and, some-times, "game time" decisions. If you offer the suggestions in that spirit, the teams responsible for execution will be more apt to support. This is a potential "be unexpected" opportunity where the receiver may share they always do something the same. We are not looking for routine, we are looking to be intentional and memorable.

c. I recall another dinner, like many that I attend, where there was limited room for interaction and the tables were arranged as long tables of fifteen. Very challenging to have group conversations.

d. Some suggestions to try:
    • Request a room with windows or close access to natural space.
    • Evaluate the lighting.
    • Evaluate the noise level (have someone audit prior to booking).
    • Is there room to move around? My recommendation, which has worked

100 percent of the time, is instead of requesting a room for the number of participants, double or triple the amount and then you will have extra space. In most cases, this does not cost extra since the fees are normally around the food and amenities (Negotiate).

- Is there an option for round tables?
- Is there an option for another area for meals?
- For the actual meeting, my preferred room set up is U-shaped, even if it is three or four levels deep. The more the participants can see each other, not just the speaker in the middle, the more engagement. Most venues' standard is classroom style, this is where pre-planning and asking for something different is effective—or come early and move the tables.
- Two cost-saving ideas:
  o Venues typically charge ten times for flip charts and accessories
    ▪ Bring your own power cords— many venues charge $25 per cord.
    ▪ Consider low-tech—instead of slides on a screen consider port-

able flip charts. I prefer ones that
are like large sticky notes, so you
can stick on the walls around the
room. I also prefer the ones that
fold like a triangle/easel and
allow you to be mobile. This
mobility can foster small group
work and a change of venue,
including moving the meeting
outdoors.

Be Unexpected Thoughts on Dining:

I am going to share some simple and actionable ideas to
increase the connection and experience. I did not grow up
with the cotillion/debutant society but was exposed early on
to multicultural restaurants, dinner parties, and work
dinners with my parents. I briefly remember taking an
etiquette class as part of a modeling program. I share these
details because this is an area I noticed I have passed the life
experience on to my children. Our daughter has planned
and executed numerous dinners for friends and coworkers
and large-scale social and fundraising events, for fun. Our
son has planned video and podcast productions.

When organizing meals for a group of four or more, it is
important to be accommodating, provide nutrition that
provides energy and focus, and it does not take a lot of extra
work to provide enjoyment or a positive experience.

- If you are doing a dinner for six people or more,

consider asking the restaurant for your name and/or logo on top of the daily printed menu (most fine-dining restaurants offer this as a service at no fee).

- Accountability and creativity for vegetarian or other special requests. Plan so people are not put on the spot. Make sure there are equal options.

- The worst example I have of this occurring: We were at a technology awards breakfast with founders and executives at a five-star hotel in a major city. We had a china-plated, $125-per-plate breakfast. I was seated at a table of 90 percent vegetarians, so I picked that option as well, and we were served a ten-inch soup bowl filled with gray, plain oatmeal—not even a sprinkle of cinnamon— and that was it! And they *still* charged $125 . . . to the bill—I inquired post-event to the organizer. With the many options available and creative chef options, there is opportunity to shine and have seen that occur as well. This is an area you cannot assume is going to be consistent across venues, so you need to ask.

- A Danish is not a breakfast for high-energy, deep-thought sessions. Consider requesting high-protein, low-sugar options. This is another area where I broke the mold and inquired other options for my team. I even offered to pay the difference myself to appease the objections.

- Another idea that has worked well, and high-value hospitality suppliers are open to working with you if you share your values of not wasting food, is ordering buffets (if you have fifty people, you order food for thirty with place settings for fifty) or specific menus for á la carte.

- For dinners I prearrange (some establishments have you sign a waiver form—I have only had one say no) with to-go boxes, since many of the attendees are away from their families and bringing home a nice meal or dessert is a win for them.

Encouraging Conversation:

Multi-course dinners are a great opportunity to establish rapport and interest with the chef or sommelier. It does not have to be a tasting menu to accomplish this scenario. This comes back to planning; you can stage toasts, comments, and topic starters all between courses using the food to gain the attention. Make the remarks short and to the point so people can go back to individual conversations. A quick break or prompt can assist people in having deeper conversations.

The Name Tag:

This is one area we can influence as leaders. In brief research on this topic, I learned that name tags were used as a form of *punishment* during the Roman era 34 AD.

I have a love/hate relationship with name tags. I have ruined more suits and purses by putting the sticker ones on them. And, for those of you with long hair, you will understand, as the corner creeps up from the sticker, it then sticks to your hair and falls off.

I want to share a few ideas on how to make name tags not a punishment but a creative outlet and engagement model:

- Bring back tent cards. A tent card is an eight to twelve-inch paper folded like a tent that the participant puts in front of them. These can be premade and used as seating cards or can be incorporated as part of an ice-breaker activity. I have one example where we provided markers and stickers (for business professionals) and they got super creative. This is helpful with meetings and dinners to remember names.

- If you choose to provide name tags for an intimate dinner or a twenty thousand-person customer conference, make something people can read. Light font on a dark background is very hard to see at a distance.

- Distinguish between categories, for example: customer, employee, analyst.

- Make the first name three to five times larger than the last name. The company name should be prominent as well.

- I have noticed consistently that most professional associations add ribbons or another flair which indicates if the person is a board member, speaker, or award winner. This is helpful for identification. This is an area where you can establish your brand, focus, and expectations with the teams executing this part of your business.

Do Your Homework (a.k.a. Research):

I grew up in the library; my father's first professional job out of graduate school was at Enoch Pratt Library in Baltimore. I have always felt at home in the research halls from grade school to grad school, and I still have an affinity for the history and knowledge being shared in this venue. Besides going to an in-person library, there are now adjacent resources ranging from live videos and audio recordings to the broad array of advanced resources for discovery in addition to 10K's, Analyst Calls, and Reports, Industry and Academic Thought Leadership, Podcast, and Video and Social Platforms.

Last Word: Bring Back the Invitation and Thank You Note

Until the postal service becomes a thing of the past, I am a huge fan of paper invitations and handwritten thank-you notes. There is no substitution, and the main objection I hear is "I have bad handwriting." Well, so do I and 75 percent of the population, but do it anyway. *Be Unexpected.* The digital communication is great, but it fades quickly. Thank-you cards are the best way to bring something to an end and begin a new chapter in the relationship.

Human Intelligence Research Resources:

- Randy Charles Epping's *The 21st Century Economy—A Beginner's Guide: With 101 Easy=to-Master Tools for Surviving and Thriving in the New Global Marketplace*

- Boardroom Insiders – Executive Engagement Solutions for ABM & Sales: https://info.boardroominsiders.com/
- D&B Hoovers: https://www.dnb.com/products/marketing-sales/dnb-hoovers.html
- ZoomInfo – B2B Database: https://www.zoominfo.com/
- Sales Intelligence Network for Enterprise Sellers: https://emissary.io/
- Delve Risk Solutions: https://www.delverisk.com/
- IBIS World Industry Trends: https://www.ibisworld.com/
- LinkedIn Sales Navigator: https://business.linkedin.com/sales-solutions/compare-plans
- Business Imperatives and Financials Databook: trydatabook.com

There are many global analyst and research firms, from universities to the private sector. Here are a few of my go-to that cross industries and geographies. I encourage you to take advantage of the research from local technology councils and chamber of commerce in addition to these global thought leaders.

- PwC: https://www.pwc.com/gx/en/ceo-agenda/ceosurvey/2021.html
- Forrester: https://go.forrester.com/research/predictions/?ut

m_source=twitter&utm_medium=social&utm_ca
mpaign=2016_aoc_cx

- McKinsey: https://www.mckinsey.com/featured-insights/download-hub
- Deloitte:
  https://www2.deloitte.com/global/en/pages/abou
  t-deloitte/articles/global-report-home.html
- IBM Global Value Institute:
  https://www.ibm.com/thought-leadership/institute-business-value/
- Milken Institute:
  https://milkeninstitute.org/explore/research-and-analysis
- Edelman Trust Index:
  https://www.edelman.com/trust/2021-trust-barometer

B-SIDES OF

BE UNEXPECTED

/////////////////// **PLAYLIST**

- **"Right Now"** by Van Halen
- **"Let's Get It Started"** by the Black Eyed Peas
- **"We Are the Champions"** by Queen
- **"Man in the Mirror"** by Michael Jackson
- **"Try Again"** by Aaliyah
- **"Welcome to Atlanta"** by Jermaine Dupri
- **"I Am Woman"** by Helen Reddy
- **"I'm Still Standing"** by Elton John
- **"Twice as Hard"** by The Black Crowes
- **"Beautiful Day"** by U2
- **"I Am The Fire"** by Halestorm
- **"Kickstart My Heart"** by Mötley Crüe
- **"Don't Stop Me Now"** by Queen
- **"September"** by Earth, Wind & Fire
- **"Kashmir"** by Led Zeppelin
- **"I Want to Break Free"** by Queen

- "The Big Payback" by James Brown
- "Smoochin'" by Mark Knopfler
- "Rhythm Is a Dancer" by Snap!
- "Dancing Queen" by ABBA
- "Bad Blood" by Taylor Swift
- "Stronger" by Kelly Clarkson
- "Firework" by Katy Perry
- "Barracuda" by Heart
- "Drive" by Incubus
- "Sunday Best" by Surfaces
- "You Say" by Lauren Daigle
- "Don't Stop Believin'" by Journey
- "If Today Was Your Last Day" by Nickelback

////////////// *BIBLIOGRAPHY*

Adams, Susan. "How Convey Power with Your Voice." *Forbes.*
November 25, 2014.
https://www.forbes.com/sites/susanadams/2014/11/25/ho
w-to-convey-power-with-your-voice/#e489ddc82e7e.

Arora, Arun, and Peter Dahlström and Eric Hazan and Hamza
Khan and Rock Khanna. "Reimagining Marketing in the
Next Normal." *McKinsey & Company.* July 19, 2020.
https://www.mckinsey.com/business-
functions/marketing-and-sales/our-
insights/reimagining-marketing-in-the-next-normal.

Bath, Amritpal. "The Story of Buttercup, the Splunk Pwny." *Splunk.*
https://www.splunk.com/en_us/blog/splunklife/the-
story-of-buttercup-the-splunk-pwny.html.

Best, Jo. "IBM Watson: The Inside Story of How the Jeopardy-
winning Supercomputer Was Born, and What It Wants to
Do Next." *TechRepublic.*
https://www.techrepublic.com/article/ibm-watson-the-
inside-story-of-how-the-jeopardy-winning-supercomputer-
was-born-and-what-it-wants-to-do-next.

Black, Erin. "Meet the Man Who 'Invented' the #Hashtag."
CNBC. April 30, 2018.
https://www.cnbc.com/2018/04/30/chris-messina-
hashtag-inventor.html.

Brunsman, Barrett J. "P&G Resurfaces Ad Effort as New
Campaign on Race Relations Launches." *Silicon Valley
Business Journal.* June 8, 2020.

https://www.bizjournals.com/sanjose/bizwomen/news/latest-news/2020/06/p-g-ad-on-race-relations-generates-massive-views.html.

Burchard, Brendon. *High Performance Habits: How Extraordinary People Become That Way.* Hay House Inc. 2017. pg. 252-3.

Burkus, David. "If You Want to Be the Boss, Say 'We' Not 'I.'" *Harvard Business Review.* March 6, 2015. https://hbr.org/2015/03/if-you-want-to-be-the-boss-say-we-not-i.

Caple, Jim. "How MLB Walk-Up Music Became a Designated Hit." *ABC News.* August 31, 2015. https://abcnews.go.com/Sports/mlb-walk-music-designated-hit/story?id=33437245.

Carnegie, Dale. *How to Win Friends and Influence People.* Simon and Schuster, 1936.

Clair, Michael. "Here's How Walk-Up Songs Went from Organ Tunes to a Cultural Sensation Almost Overnight." *CUT4 by mlb.com.* July 10, 2019. https://www.mlb.com/cut4/the-complete-history-of-the-walk-up-song.

Cuddy, Amy J.C. *AmyCuddy.com.* https://www.amycuddy.com.

Dallas, James H. *Mastering the Challenges of Leading Change.* Wiley, 2015.

Fletcher, Molly. "About Molly." *MollyFletcher.com.* https://mollyfletcher.com/about.

FranklinCovey. "The 7 Habits of Highly Effective People." *FranklinCovey.com.* https://www.franklincovey.com/the-7-habits.html.

Heinecke, Stu. *StuHeinecke.com.* https://stuheinecke.com.

Humphrey, Judith. "Six Steps to Speaking as an Authentic Leader." *The Humphrey Group* (blog). December 8, 2015. https://humphreygroup.com/blog/2015/12/8/six-steps-to-speaking-as-an-authentic-leader.

Humphrey, Judith. *Taking the Stage.* Jossey-Bass, 2014.

Jenkins, Tiffany. "Why Does Music Evoke Memories?" *BBC Culture.* October 21, 2014. https://www.bbc.com/culture/article/20140417-why-does-music-evoke-memories.

King, Martin Luther Jr. "'Levels of Love' Sermon Delivered at Ebenezer Baptist Church." *Stanford University.* September 16, 1962. https://kinginstitute.stanford.edu/king-papers/documents/levels-love-sermon-delivered-ebenezer-baptist-church.

Krockow, Eva M. "How Many Decision Do We Make Each Day?" *Psychology* Today. September 27, 2018. https://www.psychologytoday.com/us/blog/stretching-theory/201809/how-many-decisions-do-we-make-each-day.

Lenzner, Robert. "BlackRock's $6 Trillion and The Social Purpose of Corporations." *Forbes.* January 17, 2018. https://www.forbes.com/sites/robertlenzner/2018/01/17/blackrocks-6-trillion-and-the-social-purpose-of-corporations/#186b1652a1e6.

LinkedIn, *LinkedIn Sales Navigator,* https://business.linkedin.com/sales-solutions/cx/18/08/linkedin-sales-navigator?src=go-pa&trk=sem_lss_gaw&veh=LSS_NAMER_T1_US_Search_Bing-Brand_DR-PRS_Contextual_SalesNavigator-Alpha_All_English_Core__linkedin%20navigator_e_c__&mcid=6621213424619700239&cname=LSS_NAMER_T1_US_Search_Bing-Brand_DR-PRS_Contextual_SalesNavigator-Alpha_All_English_Core&camid=329654293&asid=1283130213181589&targetid=kwd-80195739249536:loc-190&crid=&placement=&dev=c&ends=1&gclid=4b0911712329128dc8417156f6084de5&gclsrc=3p.ds&msclkid=4b0911712329128dc8417156f6084de5&utm_source=bing&utm_medium=cpc&utm_campaign=LSS_NAMER_T1_US_Search_Bing-Brand_DR-PRS_Contextual_SalesNavigator-Alpha_All_English_Core&utm_term=linkedin%20navigator&utm_content=linkedin%20navigator.

LinkedIn. *The LinkedIn State of Sales Report 2020.* https://business.linkedin.com/sales-solutions/b2b-sales-strategy-guides/the-state-of-sales-2020-reportMcLeod &

More. *McLeodandmore.com.*
https://www.mcleodandmore.com/.

Markoff, John. "Computer Wins on 'Jeopardy!': Trivial, It's Not."
The New York Times. February 16, 2011.
https://www.nytimes.com/2011/02/17/science/17jeopard
y-watson.html.

McSpadden, Kevin. "You Now Have a Shorter attention Span
Than a Goldfish." *Time.* May 14, 2015.
https://time.com/3858309/attention-spans-goldfish.

Miller Heiman Group. "Move the Deal Episode 15: Neil
Rackham Reflects on 50 years of Bringing Science to
Sales." *Miller Heiman Group* (blog). October 2, 2019.
https://www.millerheimangroup.com/resources/blog/mo
ve-the-deal-episode-15-neil-rackham-reflects-on-50-
years-of-bringing-science-to-sales.

Morrin, Amy. *13 Things Mentally Strong People Don't Do: Take
Back Your Power, Embrace Change, Face Your Fears, and
Train Your Brain for Happiness and Success.* William
Morrow, 2017.

Nagy, Emese. "Newborn Smiles Aren't Just a Reflex—Scientists
Are Finding Babies Can Respond to Social Interactions
From Birth." *Newsweek.* November 1, 2018.
https://www.newsweek.com/newborn-smiles-arent-just-
reflex-1196077.

Psychology Today. "Emotional Intelligence." *Psychology Today.*
https://www.psychologytoday.com/us/basics/emotional-
intelligence.

Rackham, Neil. *NeilRackham.com.* http://neilrackham.com.

Raines, Laura. "Dramis' Vision: Technology that 'Adds Value,
Changes the Dynamic.'" *Atlanta Business* Chronicle.
October 26, 2016.
https://www.bizjournals.com/atlanta/news/2016/10/26
/dramis-vision-technology-that-adds-value-
changes.html.

Raising Children. "What's In a Smile?" *RaisingChildren.net.au.*
https://raisingchildren.net.au/babies/connecting-
communicating/bonding/whats-in-a-smile.

Raymond, Joan. "How to Choose the Best Seat in a Meeting Every Time." *Today.* April 6, 2017. https://www.today.com/health/how-choose-best-seat-meeting-every-time-t110087.

Rice, Curt. "How Blind Auditions Help Orchestras to Eliminate Gender Bias." *The Guardian.* October 14, 2013. https://www.theguardian.com/women-in-leadership-/2013/oct/14/blind-auditions-orchestras-gender-bias.

Ross, Lorrie Thomas. "I JUST Wish Women Would Stop Saying Just!" *Wild Web Women.* https://wildwebwomen.com/i-just-wish-women-would-stop-saying-just.

Russell, Joyce E. A., "Career Coach: The Power of Using a Name." *The Washington Post.* January 12, 2014. https://www.washingtonpost.com/business/capitalbusiness/career-coach-the-power-of-using-a-name/2014/01/10/8ca03da0-787e-11e3-8963-b4b654bcc9b2_story.html.

Sadler, Melody A., and Sei Jin Ko and Adam D. Galinsky. "The Sound of Power: Conveying and Detecting Hierarchical Rank Through Voice." *Association for Psychological Science.* 2014. https://journals.sagepub.com/doi/abs/10.1177/0956797614553009.

Sergeant, Desmond Charles and Evangelos Himonides. "Orchestrated Sex: The Representation of Male and Female Musicians in World-Class Symphony Orchestras." *Frontiers in Psychology.* August 16, 2019. https://www.frontiersin.org/articles/10.3389/fpsyg.2019.01760/full#:~:text=10.3389%2Ffpsyg.2019.01760-,Orchestrated%20Sex%3A%20The%20Representation%20of%20Male%20and%20Female,in%20World%2DCl ass%20Symphony%20Orchestras&text=This%20study%20examines%20the%20representation,in%20world%2Dclass%20symphony%20orchestras.&text=Significant%20differences%20in%20representation%20between%

20orchestras%20of%20the%20three%20regions%20are
%20reported.

Solely Original. "It's Shoesday!!!" *SolelyOriginal.com.* May 24,
2016.
https://solelyoriginal.com/blog/index.php/2016/05/24/the
-10-best-shoe-quotes-of-all-time-2.

Speakeasy Inc. "The Power of a Woman's Voice."
Speakeasyinc.com.
https://www.speakeasyinc.com/womans-voice.

Tannen, Deborah. "The Power of Talk: Who Gets Heard and
Why." *Harvard Business Review.* September 1995.
https://hbr.org/1995/09/the-power-of-talk-who-gets-
heard-and-why.

The Magis Group. *The Magis Group, LLC.*
https://www.themagisgroup.com.

Tony Robbins. "The Platinum Partnership Experience." *Robbins
Research International, Inc.* 2020.
https://www.tonyrobbins.com/platinum-experience.

Transformational Leadership. *Transformleaders.tv.*
https://transformleaders.tv.

Van Edwards, Vanessa. "How to Pick the Right Seat in a
Meeting EVERY Time." Science of People.
https://www.scienceofpeople.com/seating-arrangement.

Vision Pursue. *VisionPursue.com.* www.visionpursue.com.

Walker, Sam. "When Violence Erupted, One Mayor Found All
the Right Words." *The Wall Street Journal.* June 6, 2020.
https://www.wsj.com/articles/when-violence-erupted-
one-mayor-found-all-the-right-words-11591416001.

Wikipedia. "Neil Rackham." Last modified September 9, 2020,
21:54. https://en.wikipedia.org/wiki/Neil_Rackham.

Wikipedia. "Tyra Banks." Last modified September 15, 2020,
14:41. https://en.wikipedia.org/wiki/Tyra_Banks.

Zhu, Juliet, and Jennifer Argo. "Exploring the Impact of Various
Shaped Seating Arrangements on Persuasion." *Journal of
Consumer Research.* 2013.
https://papers.ssrn.com/sol3/papers.cfm?abstract_id=222
8843.

Motivators

Blalock, Becky. "DARE." *BeckyBlalock.com*.
    https://www.beckyblalock.com/dare.

Brantley, Gary L., II. *The Art of Organizational Transformation: 7
    Steps to Impact & Influence*. Gary L. Brantley II. 2019.

Greenleaf, Robert K. *Servant Leadership—A Journey Into the Nature of
    Legitmate Power and Greatness*. Paulist Press. 2002.
    https://www.greenleaf.org/products-page/servant-
    leadership-a-journey-into-the-nature-of-legitimate-
    power-and-greatness/.

McLeod, Lisa Earle. *Selling with Noble Purpose: How to Drive
    Revenue and Do Work That Makes You Proud*. Wiley. 2012.

Steele, Rickey. *The Heart of Networking*. James & Brookfield
    Publishers LLC. 2011.

////////////// *ABOUT THE AUTHOR*

Marva Bailer, MS, has a gift for human connection. She shares her insights and positive energy created through her successful career as a high-technology sales and go-to market leader. She develops talent and leads high-growth teams to be trusted advisors, innovators, and inspirators. She is a featured speaker and panelist for global conferences and podcasts. Marva has a BA in communications from the University of Maryland and a Master of Science in organizational development and change management from John's Hopkins University.